From Prostitutes Ministers and Ev

in Between

My Words, My Life, My Experiences; A

Memoir

Phil Woodford

Table of Contents

Dedication

In memory of Colin and Vale.

Acknowledgements

When I needed them the most, you were there right beside me – I can never say thank you enough, but I should try more. This is for you guys. Stay safe, stay well; we only get one chance to live, usually.

Many thanks also to Vicky Woodford, Erica Trafford; Lynne Wyre, Liz Mc-Dougall, David 'ready meals' Wilkinson Stuart Hosking-Durn, Louise and Steve Jones, Aaron Cummins, Helen Pye, Shahnaz Asghar; Vicky Seville, Claire and Andy Hale, Mum, Chris Woodford, Gertie Nicphillib, Debbie Woodford, Chorni Henriques, Simon Henriques, Grandma Sharon, Dr S. McKimmie, Kate Eady, Cara Berriman, Martin and Kayleigh, Karen Royle and Glenys Marriott, Simon Rigg, Neil Parker and Stephen Blanchard, Andrew and Jane Sullivan, Dr Shahedal Bari; all of the Huggett Suite at the RLI, Dame Jackie, Beth 'Angel' Airey, Dr P Atkinson, Shyam Kumar, Ian 'rev' Dewar. David 'my' cleaner at the RLI… that's some easy book sales ☺.

And last but not least, my beautiful family, who deserve much better than me: Shana, Kids, and little Leera.

About the Author

Phil Woodford (50) lives in Lancashire, Northwest England with his wife, Shana, two daughters and a Greek rescue dog called Leera. He is passionate about equality and excellent customer service. Phil grew up on the outskirts of Liverpool in a new town called Skelmersdale. He has worked for the English National Health Service since 1999 in several senior management roles leading to his current role as a Director at an acute hospital NHS Trust. Phil is a Chartered Marketer and dreams once again of running his own business, whatever that may be. He spends his spare time reading, walking and cycling, although that has become less and less following him surviving an extensive Stroke in 2016 which has left Phil with several disabilities and long term conditions.

Phil is very open about his mental health problems which he believes along with his physical illnesses, were all preventable and resulted from adverse childhood experiences (ACE). Phil also undertakes voluntary activities where he is currently the Chair of a local NHS Stroke and Neurological Patient and Carers Assurance Group for the Lancashire and South Cumbria Integrated Stroke Neuro Delivery Network. Phil regularly dreams of retirement in the Netherlands, aimlessly cycling around back lanes all day long, stopping at coffee shops to write and watch the world go by and hopefully at least one pain-free day – something that has alluded him for maybe a decade more now.

Health Warning

I swear a lot, including when I write. I've toned it down slightly for this work, but if you don't like swear words, please read with caution.

Note:

Where necessary, I've used pseudonyms throughout; I've also re-told conversations and events as I remember them, but accept that I will inevitably have forgotten some of the exact words due to the passage of time and suffering a Brain Injury.

Introduction: Daydream Believer

I woke up to the morning sun shining in through the floor to ceiling windows, which were a nightmare to keep clean. My legs weren't stiff this morning, and it had been over a year since I'd needed a walking stick. Such was the change in my daily routine.

New York in the spring is always my favourite time of the year. The parks are starting to bloom, and the kids are out playing in the streets and parks; boisterous noise filled the air.

The City had just begun to come alive after the Christmas craze. It was Friday, and I had the day off. A few hours remained yet before the family were 'zooming' with me, amidst the new 'normal' since Covid. Some things had stayed in place, though. I felt the excitement of the Zoom call building up inside me. I missed them all like mad. I had to be away from them, though, because the offer of working in New York was a 'once in a lifetime opportunity'. Too great a chance for me to run back and regress to an old way of life.

The din of the traffic had begun to become comforting as the days then months went by. I didn't even notice it sometimes. Living just a stone's throw away from the bridge had its challenges, along with an endless supply of tourists, smog and traffic chaos. I got out of bed, stretched on the soft exercise mat and breathed in the coffee smell wafting in from the kitchen, and went and poured myself a mug.

I'd adjusted to sharing an apartment, mainly as Lewis was stinking rich. I could never in my wildest dreams afford a place like this. Living in 'Dumbo' (Down Under Manhattan Bridge Overpass) was becoming expensive now that Etsy and the Hipster crowd it employed had started to move in all around me. Lewis and I were once the only people in the converted warehouse six months ago, and now we were part of a shared community of 500. I sat in front of the window in my Conrad-Esque red Pod egg chair, pretentious – Moi? I've always been a daydreamer. I sat there for a while, sipping the coffee, pondering the secret of my success.

If this is the type of book and memoir/biography introduction you were looking for, move on and read another, this isn't it.

I am not a 'successful' or a rich person; I've no secret or self-help tips to pass on. I'm currently seated at my kitchen table, uncomfortable and stooped over the keyboard. I live with my wife Shana, two daughters and a dog (Leera) who we rescued two years ago from Cyprus. I type with the aid of dictation software. I'm nearly six-foot-tall, which is to say I'm short enough to say I'm roughly six-foot. I'm overweight and unshaven except for my bald head. I have several tattoos on both arms and enjoy walking. However, I can no longer walk very far. I walk with a slight limp on my left-hand side and occasionally use a walking stick when fatigued. I suffer from hemiparesis, which means I have weakness down one side of my body (left) resulting from a stroke I survived five years ago. Initially, it left me hemiplegic. I was unable to move anything on that side of my body. Including my stomach and bladder muscles, I was amazed there were any muscles below the fat!

I also have a compressed nerve in my lower lumbar region that causes excruciating pain in my back, groin and down my left leg and into my foot. I have several other interrelated ailments, including arthritis... I live with the discomfort and pain from psoriasis and psoriatic arthropathy together with Ankylosing Spondylitis (AS).

AS is a long-term condition in which the spine and other areas of the body become inflamed. Essentially, I'm old, fat and falling apart. Most of my illnesses are linked in one way or another. I'm not sure if I have anyone to blame but myself?

The stroke is said to have been caused by the side effects of an anti-inflammatory medicine. I have my doubts. The pain is currently close to unbearable. At times, the pain meds don't seem to make any difference anymore, and self-medicating looks quite attractive. I developed incredible pain in my ribs recently, "Costochondritis," the doctor says. It is the medical term for inflammation of the cartilage that joins your ribs to your breastbone (sternum). Who knew this was even a condition? It turns out it's not even that uncommon. This area is known as the costochondral joint. I feel like I've been punched in the sternum and ribs, there is no bruising or swelling, yet it hurts to touch. Since Covid, I'm at the back of the list to see a pain specialist, but Glenmorangie, in small amounts, helps now and again!

"Don't point and stare, dear, it is rude," her young son did not take much notice of his mum holding her hand as she shopped in the supermarket. Instead, he continued to stare without any awareness of the discomfort it was causing me.

"Hello, don't worry, you can't catch it. Would you like to ask me any questions about it?" I asked. He shook his head, and his mother turned around, blushing. She looked at me, "I'm so sorry; he doesn't mean any offence." She stuttered.

"I know, it's okay; I would stare at me too! But, it is okay if he wants to talk to me about it. I'm happy with that, as next time he sees somebody like this, he might be more comfortable?"

"That is very kind of you," said his mother, "but he needs to learn to mind his own business." She said this in the tone that only mothers can muster while speaking to another person and telling their child off indirectly! It is an art.

Psoriasis had now covered my forehead and into my eyebrows. I hadn't realised, but I had blood dripping down past my left eye and over my cheek. I touched my face and realised there was blood and some nasty white flakes of skin on my finger.

"I have to apologise. I didn't realise it was bleeding. It sometimes happens, is not that often, I didn't notice, to be honest."

I took my tissue out of my back pocket and dabbed the blood away before going back to my shopping. "It was nice to meet you both," I told them, "but you can let him know he can't catch it as it is psoriasis, not leprosy."

I said that, but I did I feel like a leper at times. People don't come near me. The week before my friend's wedding, I could see people did not want me in their photographs with my traffic light red shiny head. I am more bothered by the embarrassment than any discomfort or pain.

At its worst, it covered at least 20% of my body.

25 years ago, it had started on the back of my right leg on the calf and then strangely spread symmetrically across my body. If I got a patch anywhere on one side, I knew that it would be exactly the same on the other side, the same shape and texture within weeks. I would have to vacuum my car every week as the carpet would be white as well. It felt like I was a character out of Doctor Who, who could shed its skin like a snake or the character Michael Gambon expertly portrayed in The Singing Detective.

People at work were excellent, though. They never mentioned this other than bringing me the latest miracle wonder cure that all of their wives had read about in a glossy magazine. Of course, none of them made any difference, but I lived in hope. Psoriasis can cause the sufferer to live a life of isolation and depression; you feel like an outcast.

Episodes like the one at the supermarket were a commonplace occurrence. Something like that happened at least monthly. It would be the same if I would be wearing shorts in the summer. My legs would be all different colours, white from the flakes of skin which would peel off, the size the size of your hand, or the bright redness it left behind as it shed. Those who suffer as extensively as I did have a higher chance of developing psoriatic arthritis, similar to rheumatoid arthritis.

I arrived at Broadgreen Hospital in Liverpool to see the dermatologist. It was a familiar routine with each specialist I met.

"Philip, could you please take off your trousers, leave your shorts on and take your shirt off and sit on the couch for me, please, whilst I examine you." The doctor would take a good look at my skin and check the movement range in my joints. "You know we are a teaching hospital Philip and I have students today... Would you mind if they also had a look, as this is quite extensive and chronic?" she said professionally.

"Of course, I am happy if that helps others to learn." I said, trying to appear professional and intellectual about the situation when I was cold and trying to think about when I could breathe out. I'm sure she realised that I was holding my stomach in, but I was quite self-conscious. I put my shirt and pants back on, and she walked through into another room while I dressed

I could hear her whispering before calling more loudly, "please take your trousers off and your shirt and come through as soon as you are ready, Philip." Why she asked me to get dressed in between, I'll never understand, slip of the mind/routine, I suspect?

"Okay." I called back, got undressed again, and in my black boxer shorts, I walked into the other room – "fuck me!" I thought, nearly saying it out loud. I could feel my penis retract in fright inside of my body!

There must have been five students, all sitting facing me with the doctor alongside them. I know it doesn't matter, but it does, really. They were all looking at me, all of them female trainee doctors. This might have been a dream and a fantasy once upon a time for me, but had I known I would have put on a new pair of boxer shorts and not my cheap-worn and slightly faded black NEXT boxers, I would have broken out the Calvin Klein's!

"Please turn around, Philip and let them see the extent of the plaque on your back." The doctor then explained my history with psoriasis and the different treatments I had tried. I was scheduled to start UV light treatments after the appointment.

"Joanne, would you mind going with Philip to the light room, where you will be able to observe the nurse applying the cream before he enters the UV pod." Joanne, the trainee doctor, asked me to follow her, which I gladly did, still breathing in so that I had a ridiculous size chest with cold man boobs!

We entered a small room with what looked like an upturned plastic bath on its end. This was an enclosed plastic 'pod' with UV lights in it. I was to sit in it for about 10 minutes with special glasses on whilst the special light did its magic. But first, they needed to apply an extraordinarily thick and pungent-smelling cream onto my sores. This was embarrassing as they used what can best be described as an ice lolly stick. The nurse gently smoothed it over the patches on parts of my body as though she was an artist painting on a canvas.

"Philip, do you have any patches on your buttocks and penis?" She asked without revealing any form of embarrassment. She made eye contact with me and smiled to help me relax. "I do, yes. Shall I pull my shorts down?"

"Yes, please, just enough so that we can get to them; Joanne sat taking notes and observing and asking me how it felt when it was applied.

"It's just a bit cold and smelly, but other than that and the embarrassment of two ladies around me. It is okay."

I was then shown into the pod, which had a plastic seat built into it. The clear door was closed behind me, and there was a button on the wall in the pod I could press if I got nervous or claustrophobic. The pod was bright white on the outside. But it looked like the inside of a smoker's lungs when I went in. It was tar-stained from the cream of other patients. Once the treatment is over, you need to shower to get all the cream off your body as it stains your clothes.

Joanne left at the end of the treatment before I showered and got dressed, and then I left to go home. I had about half a dozen light therapies over a period of time, but nothing changed or improved for me as a result. This was in about 1992, I was 22.

The only time I can say my psoriasis got noticeably better was in about 2006. I was prescribed a new biological medication, which I injected every two weeks. It was a revelation. It doesn't work for everybody, but I got lucky.

In about three months, nobody would know I once had psoriasis on my face. By six months, I could confidently say you couldn't see any on my body. I remain on the biological treatment, but since the stroke, I have had minor flare-ups, mainly on my scalp and stomach, but not to the extent of before. It does feel like a miracle.

The medication affects my immune system, which means I must have blood tests every month, to monitor its effects. I have suffered from many different infections on occasions, resulting in me being ill from shingles and swine flu. The treatment is not without its downsides, but I feel the positives massively outweigh any negatives. This is a snapshot of what it feels like to live with psoriasis daily.

I hope that reading this, you might now empathise with people with diseases, especially related to the skin. Please think twice when you see somebody with flakes of skin, perhaps on their arms. It can easily be dismissed as 'just eczema', or it's just a mild case of psoriasis, and that it's not such a severe condition. But when your skin cracks and bleeds every time you bend a joint, that's when it can be absolute agony. The loneliness and depression it causes should not be underestimated.

Why did I write this?

60,000 words later, and I'm asking myself the same thing! I wrote it just for a bit of fun. I tend to doubt myself every day, but I'm pleased now that I've written this book. It has primarily been a cathartic exercise.

I subscribe to the Ricky Gervais attitude of: "I don't give a fuck if you like what I say." Of course, he means this in the context of telling jokes and funny stories. I never set out to hurt or insult, and I am mindful I can come across as quite harsh at times.

Regardless, I do think there are a few reasons why I wrote this book. When I die, I wanted something to leave for my kids and their kids, more than money and property. I wanted to leave my thoughts. "Who was that old, fat, bald man?" they might ask. I wanted my kids and hopefully my grandkids to know me differently and not just be a picture on a family tree.

Secondly, I am regularly finding that I struggle to recall what happened this morning but can still remember details and smells from decades ago. Therefore before it all fails me, I wanted to write some of it down, preserve it, immortalise it. I thought that others might be interested. Maybe there are some things in this book for you to learn too? Time will tell on these last points.

I have got experiences to share. I enjoy recounting stories to friends and colleagues. I understand and value the power of a story. I've not set out with the ambition of making any money. If I do, great. If not, that's okay too. It seemed like a good idea on a day when I was high with emotion. Which is my challenge of living on a roller-coaster of depression, one week sad the other on a high, I currently rely on the highs to get my work done.

As a result of my love for telling a story, people have been asking me for a long time to write a book about what it's like to survive a stroke – in a nutshell, it is a pretty shit experience, to be honest! I've delivered many talks around the country on these experiences, and I quite enjoy sharing.

I was at a health conference in Birmingham two years ago. I delivered a talk with an occupational psychologist, Karen (real name). Our talk was delivered in a long narrow room at the National Exhibition Centre (NEC) in Birmingham. After my talk, a lady looking quite emotional came up to me and said, "You've given me hope, thank you. My husband, he had a stroke a couple of years ago and is quite depressed, but you have shown it is possible to recover in some way and move on."

I thought this was the zenith of my day until a second person approached me. I had casually said, please come and talk to me if you have any further questions, but I didn't for one moment think anybody would come over. They surprised me when they did!

"Can I speak to you, please?" Said a well-dressed lady clutching a notepad and pen. I initially thought it was a journalist asking for a comment or clarification on some flippant and offhand remark I had likely made about suicide. I was wrong.

"I'm a physiotherapist and social worker. Your words struck me, particularly about the need for employers to work with their employees who survive a stroke and get actively involved in their rehabilitation, and why this could be vital to their rehab and success in their return to work. I do this now, but I'm going to make sure I do more of it after listening to you on the difference it could make; thank you." It hadn't happened like this for me when I returned to work., If my employer had actively taken part alongside me with my rehabilitation, they would have understood much better my capabilities and helped my mental health and paranoia about my job security. I did try to encourage them to get hands-on; it fell on deaf ears, a bit strange, I think, seeing that I work in a hospital.

I was taken aback by the words from these two ladies. I hadn't realised I could honestly help people or be any sort of inspiration; I'm just a foul-mouthed old bloke, let alone influence another person's professional practice. I decided to take my talks a bit more seriously, so I invested in some professional public speaking training by attending a course delivered by a gentleman called Richard McCann.

Richard and I remain in contact. Richard tells a compelling and emotional story with lots of learning points. This sentence is chilling; Richard's mother was the first victim of the evil Peter Sutcliffe, better known as the Yorkshire Ripper. This moniker sent shivers down my spine as a child and must have left women frightened right across the country, not just in Yorkshire. He brutally murdered 13 innocent ladies in the mid-to-late 70s and early 80s. I would recommend people reading Richard's books about how he turned his life around after the psychological impact of this brutal incident on a young boy's life. His first book is called *Just a Boy* and is a compelling and inspirational read. Richard has had a significant impact on how I view challenges and what I can overcome and achieve.

I have also received several 'awards' in recognition of my efforts to motivate and inspire other survivors. I'm not sure I deserve any awards, but if any good can come from the stroke, I would like to think it is from helping others who have been through similar experiences, either as survivors or carers.

There's a ton of books from other survivors saying how well they've recovered. I don't find anything inspirational within my experience; I had a stroke; get over it; I have to. Unfortunately, I haven't entirely, but since completing this book, I'm feeling much brighter. I still cry most days at some memories of what has happened. Re-telling my experiences is just too painful at times, I hate the feeling. I don't have an hour, let alone a day where it's not on my mind. If you see me at work walking past you in a corridor, I'm thinking about it. In the supermarket, you get the picture, I'm sure?

Within this book, you will find a lifetime of events, experiences and views on situations that I hope you find amusing, maybe even enjoyable and valuable. My stories and thoughts will likely offend some of those closest to me. I am, for the most part, unapologetic, as only I know how I feel. I've tried only to include anecdotes that help explain who I am and why I am.

I've taken a chapter out of the book based on my notes from conversations with people, as I don't believe that they will see the events in the way I wrote them several years earlier. And I now feel more at ease about it too.

I am an NHS director working at an NHS hospital trust called University Hospitals of Morecambe Bay, NHS Foundation Trust. I am responsible for several areas, but most notably, corporate communications. I'm also a qualified Chartered Marketer, and I am currently studying behavioural economics and behavioural change, particularly habits.

I did leave the NHS once and came back after spending periods in Higher and Further Education. While these other organisations were full of talented people, they made the NHS appear fast and agile – which certainly is not in my experience. Pre-NHS and after leaving College, I seriously considered joining the British Army – I regret still that I didn't. I did a bit of research when I was 19 or 20 to join the French Foreign Legion and running away from life. It was probably for the best that I didn't!

A childhood of reading Beau Geste cartoons in the newspaper was unlikely to have provided me with the grounding I needed. And whilst now changed in terms of acceptance criteria, they are famed for once accepting anyone wanting to create a new identity and wipe the slate clean, including criminals and deserters. I found this an attractive thought to meet and live with people with such backgrounds. After dropping out of college early, I joined my dad's transport firm in a bit of a handyman role, cleaning the offices, making brews, and something I surprisingly enjoyed, cleaning the toilets! Although my wife would not recognise that skill in me now!

Some people will find fault and inconsistencies in my story, where I'll quote something happening in 1976. Still, they'll take delight in telling me that it couldn't have been '76 because, well, to be blunt, I'm not interested in armchair Google warrior researchers. They can go back to spreading conspiracy theories about Covid and 9-11. Jog on.

In preparation for writing this book, I visited tons of websites on 'How to write a Memoir', and in the end, I felt that this is my story; I'll tell it how I like. I'm not out to become rich from my writing; I don't have a 'neat' well-defined target audience in mind like the websites described these neatly homogeneous groups of people. The theory is satisfactory, but ''it won't be achieved without a huge budget, so I've set out to entertain those who are perhaps curious.

The initial themes that I wanted to write about were:

- Adverse Childhood Experiences (ACES) and how they can impact a person's health many decades later.

- My experiences of surviving a stroke when I was 45; and

- My role in response to the Morecambe Bay Maternity Scandal.

But it has morphed from a memoir into something more expansive. By the time the Editor and proof reader have finished with my words, I'm hoping that they have become legible and make coherent sense to those who choose to read them. I'm at that stage in my life where I am battling with the existential questions of "who am I" and "why am I me?" A bit like the Fantastic Mr Fox. This book might help me answer some of these questions about myself too?

The websites said that memoirs don't start at the beginning, but it seems like a bloody good place to start to me! They also advised that there are several ways of writing it; in chronological order, by theme, in the third person, by stories. So essentially, there wasn't one clear view. Many also suggested that a memoir can in part be 'made up'. This sounded a bit bizarre to me, so I've ignored them all and done my own thing, as expected! People will like it or they won't; it's that simple.

Chapter 1: Bittersweet Feelings and Brutal Honesty

Even when I was happy as a child, I was sad. Am I contradictory? Never! I just 'can't make my mind up! As long as I can remember, I have always been sad and often depressed, which isn't to say there have not been good times when I was growing up, or when I was stepping out beyond the world of my mind – there have been.

I could become low just as quickly as I could get high. I could swing like that, sensitively. I'll have moments where in an hour I could be despondent and as low as you can be, then suddenly experience extreme bouts of creativity and happiness. Living this way is tiring and wears me out. I still am like this, and I don't know how to explain it to people. Perhaps I could just show them this book in the future?

Since we're talking about my feelings and honesty, let's be honest about matters. And why not start with corporal punishment, as it is part of my past, which I think about often. I am not talking about giving this punishment, but receiving it. Let me be clear; I consider it abuse. Don't challenge me after reading the book by saying, "So you think if I smack my child on the backside, you think I am abusing them?" Yes, I do. The science may be inconclusive around the matter, but I'm unconvinced otherwise. It is demoralising and degrading to children and shows an inability to control yourself.

Due to the stances I take on many issues compared to people around me, I have always felt 'different'. I just wasn't sure what 'different' really meant to me, and perhaps a day would come where I would be 'found out'. Until that happens, self-doubt all the way!

Imposter Syndrome is what I'm referring to here. It isn't just something that impacts professional people with fancy job titles, it's been a dreadful torturous feeling that's been part of my life for as long as I can remember. A sense of impending doom, that something terrible is just around the corner, the feeling of not being good enough. I put it down to having extremely low self-esteem and confidence. I could never work out what was different, though. If life goes against me, I'd always withdraw to a dark, cold place where I would see only things in my immediate view. Everything would be ghostly quiet, and I will feel cut off. It is like looking through a tube; even the sounds around me would start to 'narrow'.

I remember 21 years back, and millennium celebrations had come and gone. We had entered 2001, the world hadn't stopped rotating on its axis because of the mysterious millennium computer bug, but my marriage was coming to an end. Kate and I had both been unhappy together for some time, and we were drifting apart due to having different interests and friends.

A huge argument had taken place, and the relationship was best described as acrimonious. Kate stood up from the sofa, crying, and left the living room– the marriage had just ended. I found myself shaking and staring at the living room radiator ahead of me and the adjacent wall with no thoughts in my head. Around eight years earlier, I had been sitting on the same floor in 2001. Then I had been crying and was being comforted by Kate.

It started with a phone call. "Phil, it is Julie, Marie's (real name) friend. I do the caring for her."

"Yes I remember. Hi Julie, how are you? What can I do for you?" My dad's third wife was Marie, who was my step-mum. She was housebound with severe breathing difficulties and rheumatoid arthritis. She had a part-time carer who was her good close friend, Julie. "I am okay Philip, but Marie is in a bad way. Could you speak to her please?"

"Of course I can. If she's there now please put her on the phone." I was shaking. I didn't know exactly what was coming, but I knew it would be about my dad and something he had done. "Hi Phil, it's been such a long time since I've seen you," sobbed Marie. She was never the most articulate of people, but she was unequivocal when she went on to speak through her tears and distress.

"It's your dad, Phil, Pat." It always made me laugh; Marie would often after saying my dad would then confirm his name as Pat, almost as though just to make sure I knew who my dad was. It was always a bit strange but quite a nice quirk too.

"… He won't stop, you know what he's like, he's waking Claire (real name) up at ridiculous hours ranting and shouting, as he did with you. I can't live with it anymore. I need your help, please. I know you fell out with him, but please help me," she begged.

Claire was Marie's daughter with my dad. She was about 12 or 13 at the most. "I will be right there, Marie," I said without hesitation.

Marie and my dad lived in Skelmersdale, about a 30-mile drive from where I lived in Halewood, South Liverpool. I arrived at the house and was thankful dads' car was not outside. I knocked on the door nervously. Julie answered the door and hugged me as she wept a little. She said, "I know Marie loves him, but your dad has gone too far this time, Philip. He has to stop. It's not acceptable."

I was calm and followed Julie into the house and into the living and dining area, where I sat at the end of the dining table. Marie shouted through from the kitchen. "Hi Phil, Claire is out, and I will be through in a moment with a cup of tea." "Okay Marie, that's fine," I shouted back.

Strangely it felt nice to be back. I hadn't so much fallen out with dad as I'd just decided to stop seeing him. Kate never really liked him either, so it was easier that way. Julie caught my eye and smiled. She brought over a laundry basket full of clothes and proceeded to busy herself by folding them on the table. Marie came through with hot drinks. She was wearing a thin cardigan.

Marie was a tall lady, almost 6ft. and of large build, a little stooped over with arthritis. She needed a wheelchair and oxygen to go out of the house. Her hair was by then grey and white and quite untidy, which was very unlike her. However, Marie had always taken good care of her appearance and had a taste for the finer things in life. She spoke with a strong and cutting Liverpool accent with an inflection of the voice to sound more well-spoken at times, 'posh' almost. But there was also an undercurrent of 'scouse' whenever she tried. She was also wearing sunglasses.

At this point, she sat down in front of me and smiled, "It's so good to see you, Philip. I've missed you. She reached over the table and held my hands, "Claire always wants to see you." I felt sad at this as I'd let Claire down by not keeping in touch with her.

I responded pointedly, "We only live 45 minutes away, Marie, but in 8 years, dad has only ever brought you all round to our house once; it takes two, you know." I paused. This was the wrong time to be sniping back at her, and I knew why she was wearing sunglasses in the middle of the day; I'd seen this before.

"Take the glasses off, please Marie, you bloody look like Roy Orbison!" I said, trying to lighten the mood. I noticed her left arm was bruised too, about 5 inches up from her wrist. She removed the glasses and sobbed, "I fell down the stairs, Philip, and when I got up, I lost my balance and fell into the wall." She lied, wiping tears from her eyes as she spoke.

Her left eye was swollen and bruised, my body felt like a thermometer with the temperature rising, but it wasn't mercury. It was hate and anger boiling up inside of my body. "Don't lie to me Marie, and he's had this coming. I'm going to fucking batter him." I got up and started to walk away. "Philip, don't go, please," she begged in a desperate tone. I wanted to go and find him. I sat back down and held Marie's hand instead; I kissed her on the cheek and told her I loved her.

She poured her heart out, along with Julie commenting too on what she had witnessed. Essentially, dad was up to his old tricks of bullying the house and hitting Marie. I have no time or respect for abusers and firmly believe they deserve a dose of their own medicine. Like most bullies, they only understand one language, and in my opinion, you can't reason with them. They will lie their way out of a situation if they can. In this instance, frighten the victim so much they would lie for them. Bullies and abusers need to be named and shamed, don't let them hide the shadows. Only make them harder to spot, it does not erase them.

I agreed I would speak to my older sister (name removed), as she always knew the right thing to do. I returned home and telephoned my sister from the phone in the living room, next to the sofa near the wall and radiator. As she lived 100 miles away, we agreed I would confront my dad, telling him it must stop. I decided I couldn't control my emotions if I saw him face to face, and I was worried about what I would do, so I decided to write a letter.

After the phone call, I lent on the wall and memories of being a child flooded back. My dad's leather belt pounding my backside brought tears of agony from my eyes; I slumped to the floor and dropped the phone. I sat there hugging myself and rocking while I cried like a baby. It did feel good to let it out. I sat there for a long time until I fell asleep.

My wife Kate came home from work and found me sat on the living room floor where I had slept. I blurted out through more tears what had happened and that I would be ok; Kate sat and comforted me. I had never really said much about my dad and how I felt. He was a charmer, and to most people, he was the good-looking, charismatic, kind man, with a bit of an air of mystery to him because he was from a country that most people knew very little if anything about.

But to me, he was the absent and abusive controlling father, who had moments of kindness, but he was always on the edge of turning. He frightened me. The letter I later wrote was short but to the point. I don't recall it word for word. Still, I explained that I considered him to be a child abuser and a wife-beater in no uncertain terms. I never mentioned that Marie or Julie had spoken with me. But, I was clear, if I ever find out he was doing to Marie and Claire what he had done to me, I would deal with it myself, along with sending information to the police and social services.

I also said he wouldn't see me again. My sister, I think, was shocked at my strength of feeling. I had never discussed my feelings with her in any depth before, and they poured out in the letter. I did also write to social services but never heard from them. Useless.

I learned decades later that life was made difficult for Claire and Marie because of the letter, and this breaks my heart for me to have been so bloody naive of the consequences. Marie kept in touch, calling me on my Birthday, and at Christmas asking me to go and visit, I also received several cards and letters from my dad, I never read any of them. It had turned out to be a mistake, sending the letter. I've always gone with my gut, and I ignored it this time. I should have told what I had written to his face. I never really spoke to him again for the best part of a decade.

Claire/Marie (RIP)

I am deeply sorry, Claire and Marie, I let you both down when you needed me the most. I hope Claire, you can forgive me. I love you so much, ever since I held you as a newborn baby. I grew up with you through your funny toddler years, and I've now seen you bloom into an incredible beautiful mother and wife. On those days of sunshine, you can be confident that it is because your mum is looking down on you from heaven, smiling the proudest smile anyone could give. I know you also loved your dad very much, and I respect that. This book will hurt to see my strength of feeling. But I know it won't surprise you as you know how I feel and what went on. Don't ever blame yourself, sweetheart.

I continued to stare at the wall, where I had once sat, crying like a child. Finally, I got up and packed a bag and left. I didn't have a plan. There wasn't another woman waiting for me. I pulled into the motorway services at Burton Wood near Warrington, and I telephoned my friend Craig to tell him what had happened. Craig worked with me at the Ambulance service, and we had become quite close friends, and he was also having marriage problems.

"Mate, sorry to hear that; you okay driving? Go and Sleep in the office tonight. Janet won't be happy if you bunk down here. We can sort something out tomorrow, Phil," he reassured me. He sounded strangely excited. The morning came, and Craig came into my office at the Ambulance service. I had made a bed on my office chair with my feet on the desk. I was tired and smelly. "I've done it, Phil; I've left Janet!"

I couldn't believe it. I don't know if I'd given him the courage or not. I knew he wasn't happy. We talked for an hour before I went to get a shower. When I returned, we talked some more and were both a little 'excited' but anxious about the future. We decided to go and find somewhere to live together. Later that day, we rented a dockside apartment in Preston, but it wasn't the bachelor life either of us imagined. Instead, we sat on the floor at night after work, drinking Beck's beer and eating take-out food. We were depressing the hell out of each other! Not so much 'Men behaving badly', more like 'Men being depressingly bad'. On our first Christmas Day, we ate our lunch of Turkey curry, sat on garden chairs using the box our TV came in as a table and more Beck's beer. We treated ourselves and had bought an X-Box. This new life lasted three months. We both met partners through work with whom we have stayed with ever since. I met Shana, and 18 years later, we got married! Craig has re-married too.

It has been difficult believing you are different and don't belong. It is a feeling I still experience to this day. A feeling that I need to prove myself in some way be that through education and having more qualifications than my peers, or through working longer hours than any colleagues could imagine or learning a new skill or hobby that sets me apart.

I've spent an enormous amount of time and money in my life trying to learn new things to fit in and demonstrate I have some value and purpose.

I'm a man and traditionally speaking, we men are not very good at expressing our feelings and talking. I'm working on doing more of both. I have been cynical in the past around the benefit of talking; however, I do feel so much better when I let it out. However, that comes with the guilt of burdening my wife with my worries. I wish I had spoken more when I was growing up. I'm not convinced, though, that in the 70s or 80s, I had the people around me to listen, believe or help. I once sat down with my dad and Marie to tell them I needed help with my weight. I was about 15, and I was explaining that I was being bullied. But I received no ideas or suggestion from either of them..

As I grew up and entered the world of work, I saw some pretty rough and impoverished areas of Liverpool and beyond. These experiences set me up well for my future life, making me value and appreciate what I had a bit more.

"Yes, Love, come in; he's just in here. She stood at the door with a headscarf, covering her hair with rollers. She also wore a baggy blue cardigan and had a plain-food stained apron on, covering the rest of her body and had light blue pair of well-worn slippers. A slow-burning cigarette was stationed in one hand, and the smell of tobacco smoke hung thickly in the house's atmosphere.

"I'm from Interlink, Love, the parcel carrier. I've come to collect a pigeon going to Brighton."

"Ah yes, Derek is in here, come through." I followed her with my clipboard, packaging and a portable barcode scanner as I stepped into the door. Not only did it smell of cigarettes, it also smelled of old chip frying oil. There were no carpets on the floor. The hallway was completely bare except for a solitary black and white wedding photograph on the wall and rosary beads and a wooden crucifix hanging down from a nail on the wall.

I followed the lady into the front room, again no furniture other than four rickety paint-stained dining chairs, with Sellotape wrapped around some of the legs. In the middle stood an up-turned tea chest, posing as a makeshift dining table. I had never seen such poverty before, yet these were such kind people.

"Tea Love? Derek will be through with her in a moment."

"Yes please." I responded, feeling bad for taking anything from them. I had a folded card box, which when I opened, it popped out into a carrying box with air holes. The pigeons would be placed in the box for transport. I can't believe it was a legal practice, but it was.

Derek and his wife came back carrying cups of tea. They were white chipped china cups. Derek was incredibly thin and wore a black beret, with what looked like a military badge. He had on a white-creased long-sleeved dress shirt with the sleeves rolled up. Old creased dark navy trousers and black shoes (which were polished), but most notable was that large parts of his nose were missing, and it was black I assume from nasal cancer. I would also guess it was their best crockery for visitors. I sipped my tea whilst Derek showed me the pigeon he was cradling in one giant tattooed hand. He had swallows tattooed on the backs of his hand and faded thick blue markings on both forearms.

He was very proud of his pigeon and gently placed her in the box. I sealed the box and entered the delivery details into the computer and scanned the paperwork and box. Again, there were no carpets or rugs on the floor, just a thick black paint covering the concrete floor, a gas fire was burning away. It was summer, but the house was still cold and I would imagine it always was. I knew there was another smell above the old oil and cigarettes; it was a damp musty smell.

I drank my tea, said thank you, and felt guilty taking the £11.75 in carefully counted coins from Derek. I wanted to give him the money back, and I probably could have afforded to, even on my £80 a week salary and I regret not doing so. I visited lots of homes where people had very little.

As I walked out the front door with Derek behind me, he grabbed my left hand and pushed a £10 note into it. "This is for you, lad. Take good care of her," he said strongly in a very thick Liverpool accent. It had the intonation and tone of an order, not a request! I could have cried.

I tried to give him the money back but he was clearly a bit insulted so I didn't persist. This was a proud man, whom I didn't want to insult, certainly not in his own home. I put the £10 into my pocket, but that wasn't the end of an already eventful day. There was a battered Brown Ford Cortina full of young adults parked right behind my Ford van. I tried not to make eye contact and ignored them by getting into my van and placing the pigeon box onto the passenger seat.

I turned the ignition on and started the engine before fastening the seatbelt around the box to keep her safe, The Cortina behind me pulled around and stopped abruptly in front of my van, about one car's length ahead. It didn't feel right somehow. This part of Toxteth was tough and I'd encountered trouble before just nearby. I used my right elbow to knock the door button down to lock the door. There was no central lock or electric windows back then in our vans.

At this point, three men about 20 years of age and a woman all exited the Cortina, leaving the doors wide open. The men were in tracksuit jogging trousers, trainers and T shirts, and the woman was about 25 or 30 years of age, wearing a white and red shiny tracksuit and red baseball hat, they all ran to the back of their car they tied a rope to the back of their car bumper and then attached it to my front bumper. They looked at me through the window, I was stunned. Why didn't they just smash a window and drag me out or even easier, just ask me for the keys? I'd have just handed them over! I wasn't going to die or be beaten up for a knackered old parcel van that I didn't even own. They then got back in the car. Revving their engine, they started to try to tow away. I rammed it into reverse took the handbrake off and attempted to back away, opposing the forward force.

My front bumper gave way first and the rope slid off and dropped to the floor. I flew backwards in my van and hit a lamppost. It all happened so quick but in slow motion. At the same time, it was all very surreal. The concrete lamppost fell; it landed with a thud onto the pavement, I was already back in first gear and was spinning the van around to make my exit I was on my radio. "Link 10 to base, I'm in trouble, can you hear me?"

Ruth responded over the radio, "Go ahead, Link 10. Pat, what's up?" Link -10 was my driver call sign (I also used the name Pat at the time, but more about that later).

"I've been attacked Ruth, please call the police, my address is," and I relayed the address and which collection number I was at. I drove off, screeching the tyres until I reached St Anne's police station, which was the main police station in Liverpool city centre that I knew of. I sat outside, shaking, before going into the police station and making a report. My heart was almost bursting out of my chest.

I have often reflected on that day and have had many scrapes where I have been attacked as a driver. I believe that whilst not justified, it is understandable these people lived in very difficult circumstances. I'm sure they were just trying to do their best for themselves and family, I don't wish them any harm, they could easily have hit me over the head with a bar and take in my van and parcels, but they didn't. I don't know where they think they were taking me, though!

Maybe I was meant to jump out of the van and run? I wasn't being overly brave, but once the adrenaline takes over, it is hard to think straight. I just wanted to get away and the quickest way to me seemed to be to drive away, if I could. I have worked with other drivers who haven't been so lucky and have ended up in the hospital.

These experiences, particularly of meeting Derek, have made it easy for me to communicate to people of all levels. I'm very comfortable and accepting of differences. I have, however, omitted from the book the story about the seven naked men in a house I collected parcels from! Or the Port Police threatening to arrest me, and so it goes on. I've lived a good full life of adventure, and there is much more to come yet.

Chapter 2: The Stroke

'Stroke' is a silly little word. You 'stroke' a cat or a dog it has nice connotations, but is also something that changes the lives of people in an instant. Medically speaking, it is the sudden death of brain cells due to lack of oxygen, caused by blockage of the blood flow or rupture of an artery to the brain. The impact of this can be death, and lifelong physical and mental disability.

August 5, 2016, we had my eldest daughter's birthday. Other than that it was like any other Saturday morning. I had gone out riding my bike, nothing particularly different about it. It was a great ride, everything felt good. I climbed a hill and my legs hurt but they are meant to. I told my legs to "shut up," I often said it out loud. I was scared of the idea of having a stroke. I had seen what it had done to my mum's husband, Colin. It had stolen his life. When I said "Shut up," I honestly also said, "Shut up, I'm not going to have a stroke and get ill." It was my own therapy to motivate myself up the hill and convince myself that the pain from the arthritis whilst I cycled was nothing I couldn't overcome.

I often did this, as I had heard this is what the professional cyclist, Jens Voight would tell himself in a race to overcome the discomfort. I had cycled about 30 miles that day and I've never been what you might describe as athletic. I was slowly getting into better shape. I arrived home, took a shower, got changed, and went to sit in the garden to rest with a cold drink and review the stats of my ride on my cycle computer. I started to blink as I was struggling to focus and then suddenly, there was a sharp bright light in my left eye. It was like a torch being held up to it. I initially thought it was the reflection of the sun from the screen of my cycle computer making it difficult to see. I blinked and rubbed my eyes, then came back into the house, bumping into the open patio doors.

As I walked, I was going to get a glass of water. My eldest daughter was sitting at the dining table with her friend, who was going to come with us all to the trampoline centre later as a birthday outing. The water wouldn't stay my mouth. I sat down with them at the table, started to sneeze uncontrollably, but the sneezing went on for a good minute with no let-up. This was my brain fighting back as it turned off in part of it. I just didn't realise it at the time. Every time I sneeze now, and I do sneeze more often, my family always get on edge thinking this is 'it' again.

I feel for them when it happens, I know they care. I'm very lucky, I'm always messing around and you could see they thought I was fooling around to make them laugh. I was trying to talk to them. "Are you looking forward to later?" and more sneezes followed but the sentence trailed off as slurred, drunk-like but without the alcohol. They both started giggling, thinking I was joking.

Water was also dripping back out of my mouth as I took a sip. I was worried. I started to feel dizzy and a bit nauseous, wondering if I was having a heart attack. I'm not sure what the signs were, my heart and chest weren't hurting; surely they would be if it was a heart attack, I thought? The girls were getting anxious and shuffling in their seats. They were both 11.

"Dad, are you ok? Shall I get Mum?"

"No, I'll be okay, I'm just a bit dizzy," I mumbled. I looked on the internet browser on my phone. I knew some of the signs of a stroke, I shouted for my wife and told her I think I'm having a stroke. Shana tells a different version of this story, but this is how I experienced and remember it!

After being told not to mess around, an ambulance was called. The ambulance control room person talked Shana through some things they wanted me to try. I thought it was all a farce and that nothing was wrong with me. One of the things they asked me to do was to see if I could touch my nose with each hand. My right hand went straight to the tip of my nose, my left arm and hand felt okay to me without trying, but my left eye was still a bit weak. I pretended I couldn't touch my nose.

"Stop messing and do it properly," Shana said with obvious frustration, so I did, but I couldn't touch my nose with my left hand. I wasn't messing around this time but I honestly believed I was touching my nose. Shana was telling me I wasn't, Shana told the person on the phone this information and they said they would send an ambulance. It didn't feel like a long time to me by the time the two paramedics arrived and my symptoms had mostly passed. There were stars appearing before my left eye wherever I looked. The paramedics did their checks with their machines, which did not show anything. There was nothing to be concerned about, they explained, but they were both pretty savvy and instead listened to what I have to say and decided that it might be more serious and possibly a stroke. I was wheeled into the back of the ambulance and taken to Royal Preston Hospital about 10 miles away. I felt sorry for them as my friend a paramedic had come rushing around the house once he heard and was quizzing them on what they were doing as they loaded me into the ambulance. He was just looking out for me, I know.

Long story short, the Emergency Department at Preston Hospital also performed many checks and scans, but they were unable to find anything conclusive. I now had mostly lost vision in my left eye and my left arm was weak and uncoordinated. "It could be a migraine," said a doctor. "I said to my wife, "It's not a fucking headache!""

I have since then educated myself and now know how serious a migraine can be and also its symptoms. After about six or seven hours, I eventually ended up on a trolley bed, being admitted to the stroke ward. "All a bit of a fuss over nothing." I was musing to myself. "I hope this doesn't take long. I still have that bike race to do in the morning," I said to Shana. She shook her head in disbelief but knew me well enough that I was serious. "Let's just see what happens and we can take it from there," she said sensibly.

Meanwhile, while I was being wheeled into the ward and the nurses were talking to each other about the lack of beds in the hospital and on the wards, I am a hospital manager in the local area. This was no great shock, most of the NHS operates on the margins of full capacity all of the time. So I was braced to be told I would have to sit in the corridor or go home. I wouldn't have minded either as I wasn't sick. My eyesight had now fully returned, as had the use of my left arm and as far as I was concerned, I was okay. They had confirmed to me they did not think I had had a stroke, but wanted to keep me in overnight for observation. I was taken with my wife to an empty bed in a four-bedded ward area.

The other three beds were full of really old sick people. I was standing next to the empty bed, looking around. I could feel tears building up inside of me. This was a new feeling, it was hard to describe. It was like self-pity. I didn't like it, and I didn't realise that this was now a new feeling I would experience sometimes every hour with uncontrollable tears over the next 5 years! I was wondering, "What the hell am I doing here, I'm nothing like these people."

"Excuse me," said a nurse, now standing behind me. Based on what I'd heard earlier, I think I knew what was coming. I was going home, there was "no room at the Inn," I thought. "Would you mind if we put you in another area so that somebody else could have this bed, as we are very full?" queried the nurse.

"That's fine with me. Thank you, nurse." I was able to walk with the nurse as she led me around with Shana to a room that was called the 'Physio Room'. As I stepped in, there was one empty bed which was to be mine for the night and another with a half-naked man sitting on it with a large TV on a table. I was thinking to myself, this is a store room, God help me if I really am ill, but I spotted the 21st century essential item, a plug socket, so that I could charge my phone. There was nothing in here remotely looking like it could help me if I was ill. I stayed the night – I set my alarm for 7 AM.

After brushing my teeth before sleeping, I tried in vain to have a conversation with the other patient, but he could only point at the TV and grin. The only other entertainment was that he would later on several occasions stand in the corner of the room with a urine bottle relieving himself while still watching some crap on the TV. I woke up to this view once or twice!

I was determined I was going home to take part in the bicycle race the following morning that I had entered in. It was a different race, crossing the wet sands of Morecambe Bay on a wide-tyred bike, often called a fat bike because of the size of its tyres. I had recently purchased the bike, the race was for a local cancer care charity, to raise much-needed funds – I was very excited about the prospect, the other patient was Polish and spoke no English. The conversation ended quickly!

7 AM arrived and unlike what I was 'promised' by the nurse the night before, no Dr had yet come to see me, I'm quite literal, so if somebody says they will see me first thing in the morning as part of the doctor rounds, I take that to mean as soon as I wake up, but apparently 'first thing in the morning' and doctor rounds can mean 'anything from 9 AM to 1 PM, if at all', a nurse soon explained to me. She found it funny and I can understand why, when I unreasonably explained it was awful that the Dr was not waiting there for when I woke up. I queried if there isn't a doctor sitting in the ward how can they know when I am awake to start their rounds? "The doctor comes when they are ready, not to a set timetable," she explained, I quipped back, "I must remember to be ill at the times which are convenient for the doctor then,

thank you!" It was a sarcastic tone, but I did smile and nodded a knowing nod at the nurse.

I was now awake, so I went to the toilet and then I returned to bed, tired and a little bit worried, as I knew if the doctor didn't come round today or was called away to an emergency patient, I could be here all weekend with the man urinating into a bottle in the corner of the room.

I googled for a local taxi company to take me home then remembered that there would be taxis outside the hospital. I got up and went to look for the shower. I met a nurse in the corridor outside of the room, "Is it okay if I take a shower please, but I still have a cannula in the back of my hand?" "That would be fine," replied the nurse. I didn't have any toiletries - the shower room was in the ward area that I was taken to the night before, full of all of the sick people not like me. I wasn't sick and they were still sleeping and snoring in their beds. I entered the shower room, it was quite large as it will obviously accommodate a wheelchair if needed, more of a wet room, and on the right hand side was the toilet and next to it, behind a big curtain was the shower and immediately opposite the door was the sink, with a hand gel dispenser and a large mirror. I was wearing a T shirt, baggy walking shorts and a pair of Crocs. After closing and locking the door I got undressed. I hung my clothes on a grab rail next to the toilet before using the lavatory. The orange emergency cable hung next to it and wrapped around the fold down handrail, I spotted the hand soap at the sink. I stepped into the shower at the other side of the room and turned it on. Whilst the shower rained down and warmed up, I held onto a grab rail with my right hand and stretched with my left arm to get the hand soap out of the dispenser over the sink. The blood in my M2 artery was now blocked and parts of my brain cells were dying. Different functions in my body were now switching on and off. I felt a little nauseous (I didn't know any of this at the time). My left foot slipped. My brain was trying to sort itself out and searching for blood like a hungry dog searching for a lost bone...I tried to hold on but like a comedy act, my left hand shot up in the air as the lovers tiff in my brain reached its climax and I unceremoniously ended up on my fat arse, naked on the soaking wet shower room floor in pain and sadness. I also felt acutely embarrassed that this had happened to me, slipping in the shower with water pouring down on me and after many confusing failed attempts to sit up and a bumped head later, I rolled over onto my right side like a fucking beached whale in the rain on the beach, but I don't suppose beach whales piss themselves too, do they? "Fucking hell, I think I'm dying," The lovers tiff between my brain and the fat bloody unhealthy bitch stuck in my M2 artery began to deaden my now constant cries for "help". The brain cells controlling my speech seemed to be preventing any sound coming out of my mouth. I died that day, there and then, in my own piss, whilst the water rained down upon me. I remember vividly hovering over my pitiful broken body, looking down - it was the strangest of feelings, watching myself as though I was on a TV programme. I always thought I'd go out of life like John Belushi or with a bottle of whiskey in one hand and a blond holding the other, but no I'm going to go out in my own piss naked in an NHS hospital shower room. This isn't very 'Rock 'n' Roll', I thought to myself and knew if I wanted to live I needed to do something about it. "Help!" "HELP!" HELP!" My week cries were now starting to become a bit louder. I was also able to shuffle a small way on the floor to kick the metal bin against the wall.

My banging eventually paid off.

It was just another day for Beth the ward manager and nurse, but today Beth had come to the ward early to catch up on paperwork before her shift started. Beth heard a noise faintly through the bottom of the wall where she sat working, a banging, which she'd soon discover was from a fat man banging a metal bin against the shower room wall next door with his feet, crying like a baby for help. The shower door opened and I heard an argument between the staff debating why I was in the shower alone. I was no longer looking down. I was back on the floor looking out of my own teary eyes – I cry a lot, don't I?! A nurse explained I was 'mobile' and didn't need assistance and that "He is only in the hospital for monitoring – I saw him earlier in the corridor." I was eventually winched up and hoisted unceremoniously naked, through the ward of people who, unlike me should be there. I'd seen them all the night before, now they got to see me. I was lowered into a bed on my side. I wasn't embarrassed. I was just really thankful to be found. Any feeling of embarrassment melted away with the water in my piss down the drain. I thought I was in the hoist bag still. I was with Beth but there's a pub bar behind her - I was hallucinating. My brain was seriously struggling now. I returned back to the hospital ward and I now knew there was no bar serving alcoholic drinks! I didn't go back to check but it amused me to see what I might have mistaken for a pub bar! I think it was the counter of the nurses work station and the reception area.

"I think you've had a stroke, Phil. We're going to take you for a scan." I asked if she's calling Shana, "Yes, don't worry, somebody is calling Shana." I was worried how Shana would cope driving to the hospital whilst also sorting my dog (Vale) and kids out, so whirling quickly, I then asked Beth if she'd arranged the thrombolysis medication. If I had a stroke and it was a blockage, we would be on time to administer this medication. This is the danger of a little knowledge and working in the NHS! Beth confirmed that she had already alerted the Emergency Department and they were coming down to receive me. It was amazing how much she did calmly in such a short time, and time is life after a stroke as there is a limited window of opportunity to perform certain interventions such as thrombolysis or mechanical clot retrieval (thrombectomy). One of my first significant projects when I joined my current employer was to hold a public event to explain 'tele stroke' and the impacts of a stroke and how to spot the signs. The irony of my knowledge was not lost on me, but it never prepared me for the hell that was now ahead of me. I suddenly remembered, and despite looking calm, I wasn't inside. I knew the facts and that was weighing heavily on me already.

Stroke is the fourth single leading cause of death in the UK, and around one in eight strokes are fatal within the first 30 days. When someone does not survive a stroke, it is usually due to severe brain injury affecting those parts of the brain that control breathing and the functioning of major organs such as the heart.

(The Stroke Association UK).

Everything I've read and learn since the stroke has led me to believe that this moment in my illness was the time for the rehabilitation to start, and the mental health professionals to get involved, not days and weeks or even years later. It's too late and it's not a shock what is going to happen generally, so why wait? No harm would be done by trying. I'd seen nothing to convince me otherwise, but we still treat Stroke as an old person's condition and do not try 'hard enough' to restore good quality of life. That doesn't mean people aren't trying but it feels like the second best is accepted as a treatment option and if you're old, you should be thankful you survived.

Time passed by in a blur of scans and tests until at some point, it dawned on me that they had not made a mistake and I couldn't move the left side of my body, "Bloody hell, they're not mistaken, I have had a fucking Stroke!" I told myself. Tears began for the next 5 years. I must have drifted off to sleep or passed out as I came around and woke up in the Emergency Department. I was on a trolley, holding Shana's hand and I had a drip in my hand. It was feeding me potentially life-changing medication. A nurse was talking to me and put a doctor on the telephone to talk with me. Again, I knew what was happening. I was amazingly very calm given the situation and what I'd previously been thinking about. "Don't let them drill into my brain, Shana," I said. "I don't want to be lobotomised and kept alive like a vegetable. Kill me if this happens, please, promise me!" Shana reassured me that the doctors knew what they were doing and that I should stay calm. I did as I was told! There aren't enough specialist Stroke doctors to work in all the Stroke Units 24/7 so there was a group of them that operated virtually, so in effect there was always an emergency stroke specialist available at the end of a telephone, but with a video linkup so that they could see you from their home if needed and with the technology to view the scans remotely so that they could diagnose too.

Unfortunately, the equipment wasn't working properly, so I couldn't see the doctor on the screen, but he explained they were considering what is called a thrombectomy, where in layman's terms, they remove the blood clot from the artery in the brain by sending up a device through the groin all the way to the brain where they essentially grab and retrieve the clot and bring it back down through the artery. It is a ground-breaking procedure and it can change lives in a moment. However, that's where the positive news started and ended. This was a Sunday and apparently people didn't have strokes on a Sunday afternoon, as this was just the trial service at the hospital and they didn't have the team in at a weekend who could perform it. I believe they did try to contact staff but weren't successful. It wasn't their fault. I was bitter about it, as I read the medical notes and scans a year later and I was suitable for the procedure, and I felt I could have been transferred in time by blue light ambulance to another neuro centre such as the Walton Centre in Liverpool or Salford hospital, but I accept they could only do what they could do. And they did their best. They were asked to provide a service, Monday to Friday between certain hours - so it wasn't their fault, but clearly the people who ask them to provide the service didn't see it as a big enough priority over other services to properly fund resources. I just wish it had been 24 hours later when I collapsed as the mechanical clot retrieval can be the difference between a life without disability rather than one with it. It can be that great a difference. It's strange as ICU or A&E, or even Maternity doesn't 'close' in this way. Yes there are times of severe pressure and they then use other hospitals for support. I could have been sent via blue lights or helicopter to Liverpool or Salford for the treatment, but it wasn't considered. Again, according to the my notes and no policy to do so existed.

I could not sit up. I was also on a drip, saline I assume - you don't question meds or anything when you think you're dying or seriously ill, I just took whatever they gave me. I was told I couldn't use the toilet as they needed a therapist to assess me, but they didn't work on weekends, so I pray the lump growing in my bowels didn't want to come out just yet! I was in pain. My stomach was cramping up as I really need to relieve myself now and empty my bowels and bladder. Shana was with me and I'd been given a cardboard bedpan thing to sit on and shit into, despite the fact I couldn't sit up or move one side of my body. It was entertaining for my children and I don't blame them. I would have laughed at myself if I was them too. It's strange, I had no sense of embarrassment. Just the relief I could soon poop now, but alas it was only the thought that was giving me any relief, as I could not find a way to get up onto the cardboard bedpan.

I started to fall off the bedpan, "Which fucking idiot invented this?" I said out loud, and I bet nobody here with no muscle control has used one either! I gave up, the pain was just too bad; I don't think I was able to go to the toilet for another two days. I made excuses about not being hungry and sipped water from a cotton wool bud which also helped my lips which were now drying out. I just wanted to make sure I didn't fill my bowels or bladder up any further. I couldn't take the discomfort or the pain. It really is very short-sighted. I could have had the stroke because of high blood pressure and being hydrated can lower blood pressure, so it is a bit self-defeating and harmful to put in systems in place such as no staff to assist with toileting at a weekend, even a portable commode would have been preferable and a joyous experience it must be? As every time I came across a problem I would try to think of a solution and think I had invented something to change the world for patients in a similar situation but only to be dashed when I went on the Internet on my phone to find the products already existed, I thought I had invented. So, I can only believe it is a cost issue, or nobody in authority has tried out the equipment themselves? My inventions, which turned out not to be inventions as they already existed but never featured in my care included:

Beds that automatically weigh the patient – I was usually weighed in a wheelchair on the type of scales I used to use in a warehouse – not very dignified I thought.

Wireless automated blood pressure pulse and pulls oximetry devices. I can do all of this wirelessly at home, but apparently in a hospital, automation, Bluetooth and wireless devices have yet to be discovered - bizarre it would be so much more efficient.

Beds with built-in toilet facilities – this is one of my more bizarre ones.

Urine bottles with a one-way flow valve and turn the urine into gel - I made one when I started driving again, using wallpaper paste and scissor!

Height adjustable sinks, so that I didn't have my legs bashed into them in a wheelchair every time I was wheeled to the sink.

Beds with built-in washing facilities.

My plea would be, don't provide any equipment to patients you haven't tried yourself, maybe if you work in a hospital set up a 'testing team' of people, shouldn't be too difficult? There is a good reason medication goes through a trial and approval process, this should be the same for all equipment but with the person purchasing it also trying it out, but in the environment, and not taking it home to do in the privacy of their own home - it's a false feeling. In previous years, I have had the pleasure of getting to know a nurse called Claire who had devised an item to reduce pressure sores from nasal tubes and my colleagues all tried it out for the day so that they could assess the comfort. This was a big deal at the time, as it's not something you see regularly, but it took a nurse with compassion and insight to really put the patient first and say I am not going to give you something I haven't tried myself, she rightly won an award for this work.

Chapter 3: Moving Hospitals

I should explain that I was initially admitted into Royal Preston Hospital, following my mini undiagnosed TIA which is a good hospital. Some people thought I have a problem with it, I didn't and still don't – the people there saved my life, I'm now thankful for that, my family continue to receive great care from them too.

I feel, however, there were issues with my initial treatment. I should have been transferred to a hospital that had capacity and once diagnosed I should have been transferred to a near-by hospital that could perform the treatment. I thought fighting the Stroke treatment legally would only make me further ill rather than cure the Stroke. I did arrange for a Stroke specialist at a regional specialist stroke centre to review all of my care too. I currently live between Royal Preston Hospital and the Royal Lancaster infirmary (where I am still employed). I was frightened and despite the daily visitors, I felt very lonely there. I started to worry about the cost and stress on my fiancé of travelling every day to see me. I believed I needed to be around people I knew.

I also feared being moved further away to a rehabilitation unit in Chorley, about another 10 miles south, making it more difficult and expensive for my family to visit. I think hospital managers, underestimate the importance of access –

we rightly expect the care to be bloody good, but 'good' is made up of many parts for a patient and their family, from parking through to the quality and price of the coffee! I believe quite strongly that people in my senior position should demonstrate their trust and belief in their colleagues by receiving care where they work. I'm sure the directors of Virgin Atlantic don't frequently travel to the USA on BA! I wouldn't recommend Royal Lancaster Infirmary to other people if I wasn't prepared to use its services myself, along with that of my children. The latter have been treated at the Royal Lancaster Infirmary on a number of occasions and to a very high standard.

It is the biggest compliment I think I could pay my colleagues by being transferred there for the rest of my treatment. I spent just over one week at Preston Hospital. I badgered my colleagues via text and calls, including the directors, to help me move hospitals. Eventually somebody pulled the right strings, and I was transferred by ambulance to the Royal Lancaster infirmary. I knew and respected, Linda Dunn the clinical lead nurse for stroke services at Lancaster and felt very confident I would receive really good care under her leadership, and mostly I was right. The challenge with healthcare is that it involves people and as people we do silly things at times, and not intentionally. We're human and therefore fallible. Remember, "To err is human".

It must have been difficult for the staff on the stroke ward, as while I am not someone particularly special, I carry the fancy title of 'Director'. Like with any other job, my day-to-day office colleagues are also my friends... They all just happened to be members of the Trust Board. In the early days of my admission to Lancaster, the ward staff, bless them, had to put up with regular visits from the Trust Board members.

They breathe the same air and poo the same waste like the rest of us, but like in any job there is a little bit of nervousness when the CEO and other bosses visit the shop floor. People want to do their best and be seen doing it which is natural. It must have put the staff a little bit on edge. There was a plus side for me as I received good insight from the staff. They hadn't seen many of the board members before and so regularly kept asking me things like "Who is that?" They would ask for "What's the Chief Executive really like?" I gave honest answers. I always will. The greatest job as a leader I believe is to support others to do their job. Mostly people don't need to be told how to do a job in my experience. They just want some support which gives them confidence and the next time they will do even better!

Three and a half months were spent in that hospital. A lot happened, and again, nothing happened. I'm not going to repeat a blow-by-blow description of what happened, just some notable highlights, but I would like to share mainly with anybody who has had a stroke or has a family member or friend in a similar position. I was asked by several people to write a blog on my experience, but I refused to act as a 'spy in the camp' but I did keep some notes on my phone of things I didn't want to forget as I honestly thought It was all a kerfuffle and I'd be walking in days! I believe a lot in my own ability, a bit too much at times.

Hospital and rehab were the strangest of experiences. I was 45 and surrounded by people who looked like this was the 'last throw of the dice' for most of them. The environment in either hospital was not suitable for the mental or physical needs of survivors of a working age or younger. I'm glad they've since improved in Lancaster, but still a long way from where I'd like to see them.

"Dear nurse/doctor

My message to staff is this is just another day to you, but I've never been a patient before. This is my first time since I was a baby, needing somebody to take me to the toilet and wipe my backside. My dignity has gone, I have never been fed since I was two years old by anybody else, but you do this every day for others. I don't know what the button is for that you've given me to press. If I want a biscuit and a cuppa, do I press it? If I want my slippers, shall I press it? What's it for.

I'm not necessarily worrying about the things you think I am because nobody has spent the time to ask me. My biggest worry today as what happens if I have an erection and a nurse walks in. Please remember we are only human and scared, and we have feelings. Your curtains do not prevent us from hearing your concerns about our health or the problems of others. This is just another day for you, but to me it feels like the end of the world.

What time should I get up for breakfast? Do I let you know the night before what I want or in the morning? How do I do that? Please remember this is my first time. I don't know what to do. By the things you say, you take things for granted, meanwhile, I don't know any of your acronyms and I don't know what any of the medication is that you've given me. You've never told me what the side effects are. Write them down for me. Please take the time to tell me. I'm frightened and worried. I feel stupid. Please help me.

Will my wife leave me now that I am disabled and can't go to the toilet on my own? Will my children hate me for spoiling their lives? Please remember you drove here to work today I may never drive again. I am worried, will my boss sack me? Will I lose my home if I can't pay the mortgage? This is what is really frightening me. I'm putting on a false smile as I'm scared and don't want to look weak. Please remember I have never been a patient before, but you see patients every minute of the day; this is not new for you. Please don't stick your needle in my arm without telling me your name. You know my name, you know what I eat out;

often I go to the toilet you even know what colour my poo is, I don't know anything about you. Little things make a big difference, please take the time to tell me your name and talk to me. I had never done this before. This is my first day. I'm learning as I go along please take the time to remember. Mostly you are brilliant, but just occasionally you forget and it hurts.

It might be a nuisance for you, but I need to charge my mobile phone. I still need to pay my bills whilst I am in here and now but I can't speak properly. I can't even utilise my phone banking. This is all very confusing and difficult. Please don't give me another questionnaire asking that I recommend this service to a friend or family member. What a fucking stupid question. This isn't a shop. Ask a question you can do something with. Of course I wouldn't wish this on anybody, why would I recommend it?

My request is take greater time to explain things and to understand. Time is all we have, and potentially we have less of it than you, don't be a sheep, be a leader of the pack. It is all about choice. What choice are you going to make?"

***

"Have you got the cancer dear?" One of the patients had said to me.

It was a Saturday night, and on Stroke Ward 23 in Lancaster, we were lined up in our huge supportive armchairs in front of the flat screen wall mounted TV watching Strictly Come Dancing. Judge Rinder was one of the main stars of the show we were watching. Now, the TV is in the main communal ward area near the nurses' station. I had two old ladies to my left debating which of them would die first and which of their children had already died. This went on for about an hour throughout the programme. It was becoming nauseating and depressing to listen.

"No, I don't 'have 'the cancer', I've had a stroke" – she looked back at me, amused. "Haven't we all, but the cancer we've both had and survived. What do you think about that?"

"I er, don't really know what to say. I'm very sorry to hear that you've both had cancer, but pleased to know you've survived it." I looked away, thinking surely that would be the end of this inane questioning and the strange small talk. Not the smartest of me, I know. And then they asked about children and had any of mine died yet?! And so it went on.

"Fuck me, someone kill me now," I wanted to shout out loud but didn't. My tolerance levels were at an all-time low – I was so tired and drifting in and out of sleep now. I couldn't listen to this chatter much longer. Thank God that I had social media to browse through so I could ignore them. Thoughts and memories would come and go in the hospital, particularly of my childhood.

He said to me, "If I end up shitting into a bag Phil, you're to promise me you'll do the right thing and kill me?" I was 18, naive and I loved and looked up to my best mate like a brother. I agreed to do it for him; after all, we were best mates. Bob was a little older than me and cool. We'd hang out listening to Bowie and watching MTV in his bedroom - he was the only person I knew in the 80s with Satellite TV and access to porn TV!

"I'm going to Vancouver next week, Bob, want to come?" He booked it right away, flying out the week after me to stay with me my at my girlfriend's house in Richmond. BC, (my first wife-Kate) Bob and I made a pact one day that if we became really ill, we'd kill the other and not let them suffer. Bob had colitis this was the pre-Google era; I only knew what he told me and it sounded scary. He was a big built man, strong and muscular.

Bob and I were in a bar one night talking with some girls I knew, and we both wanted to get to know them better! Bob was looking agitated and distracted; suddenly he turned and walked off following some lads outside. The girls drifted away, leaving me cuddling my pint of beer alone! Bob came back 10 minutes later, holding his stomach tightly. I noticed he had blood on his Polo shirt near his belly button. He said it's nothing and "it was from a fight outside and someone cut me with a blade" (it was a bit rough at times, so I wasn't that shocked). I now wonder if he was lying and already had a stoma fitted and it had become infected, perhaps. He, of course, could have been just telling the truth.

These memories were coming to me as the two elderly ladies on the ward continued depressing me, so I rang my mobile bell that the nurse had given me in case I needed anything. Judy, the ward sister, pushed me back to my room. "I've had enough TV, Judy I'm really tired, can you help me to bed please." I lied, Judy agreed and helped me go to bed. I was genuinely scared. I hadn't seen Bob since I was 18 years and wondered, what if he found out I was ill and came and killed me? I'm just being silly, I told myself and I tried to meditate and control my breathing.

I wasn't sure if euthanasia is what I wanted any more. I did for a long time after the Stroke, yes. In the hospital, I wanted to die. And I believe, that day on the floor, Phil died as this Phil isn't like the old Phil and I hate that and myself for it. I'd have been better off staying quiet on the floor, the kids would have now a dad who could do all the things I wanted to do with them and he wouldn't be so moody and impatient like I am now.

At one point, I had looked to the left at the windowsill, something was moving in the corner of my eye. Fuck me if it wasn't that smart little mouse Stuart Little! He was on the windowsill next to my bed walking slowly along it and smiling, he was wearing smart green trousers; a plain white shirt and a mustard coloured felt waistcoat and a black hat.

He looked very dapper and was also twirling a cane as he walked. I felt really warm and happy at that point on my bed, but my heart was now racing.

He was initially comforting, but I soon realised this wasn't completely normal. I grabbed the nurse call buzzer with my right hand, just in case I needed it. I don't know what I thought was going to happen; I knew I wasn't going to be attacked by a cartoon mouse! But a bad feeling was coming over me like a suffocating blanket. My heart started to pound.

Looking up, I forgot about Stuart. Instead, there was a growing black cloud coming out of the ceiling with two red dots for eyes like LEDs. It grew into a large mass and two large jagged black arms and hands stretched out to me. "This is the end, I thought, this is what death looks like. I wasn't frightened, I was angry; I became cold and was shaking a little bit. Hemiplegic or not, this wasn't how I was going out, dragged off by some Demon from a dirty ceiling whilst the cartoon mouse watched on, not likely you fucker!

I looked away and Stuart Little smiled at me before disappearing as quickly as he had appeared, the black mist had also gone. My mobile phone was on the bed next to me. I quickly messaged Shana, I didn't tell her the full story of events but I texted her my DNAR instruction. I had a feeling this 'was the end not like an anxiety-induced feeling. It was different, it was more. I knew for certain what was happening but didn't want to believe it, but I knew it to be true. I also knew that I didn't want to go on living if I became worse and had another stroke, I already couldn't wipe my own arse, sit up, walk or use my left arm. If I became worse, I'd just be a burden to my family. So I asked Shana to make sure that if I needed resuscitating that they would just let me be and go live with the mouse in peace. I never pressed the buzzer. How would I explain this, when I couldn't quite explain it to myself?

Over the next few months, I did what I could to gain some strength back. First, it was my left ankle, then left foot and lower left leg where I started to get some movement. Just tiny millimetres at first – it wasn't all down to me. I had physio treatment on most days to help me regain some strength and try to re-train my brain to use other parts of it. I arranged with the doctor to have a set of electric assisted cycling pedals put next to my bed so I could be wheeled in the chair to them allowing me to exercise and feed the brain helping it to recover. I was hungry for information and found lots of information online about how exercise produced chemicals that the brain uses to heal and recover from injury, if I could find this information so easy, why wasn't there exercise equipment in my hospital room? I've seen soldiers going through rehabilitation after battle injuries and harnesses to keep them steady on a treadmill, I wanted this, but it doesn't exist where I was.

I could feel the weight piling on my body. I was always so hungry and really worried that this would affect my recovery. This particular exercise gave me a lot of hope that I could recover. I also knew from reading how beneficial exercise was to brain recovery, so it seemed – no pun intended but – a no-brainer to me why weren't the doctors and nurses giving me more exercise to do? I found a scientific article demonstrating the benefits of electrically assisted cycling in stroke rehab. I talked about it with the doctor and therapists and the possibility of a proper exercise bike for my room, but they were worried as I still couldn't sit. I thought I could overcome that issue somehow. There must be a way, a harness or brace perhaps, I thought. People with no arms and legs can do lots of amazing things so this simple thing must be possible, I told myself! I'm still convinced that only I know what I can achieve, and it is a lot more than they were giving me credit for. And this is what happens when you're in a ward mainly inhabited by elderly people, many who possibly couldn't exercise before their stroke.

Looking back, of course I know why they didn't provide any of that. You must take these things gradually so that you don't cause more damage than good. The NHS is risk averse, scared of litigation and the worry that patients actually know better – imagine! Regardless of their opinion, I kept at the exercise. If I was on my bed I would do leg lifts and hip thrusts, each time trying to do one more than the time before until I was too tired or too pained to do any more.

I came up with a game. I would place cardboard bedpans on the hospital room floor upside down one to begin with, then one more than the last each time. I'd be sat in a chair in front of it and extend my left leg up until I could put my ankle on the top of it. Each time I'd put another on top making it taller and a little bit harder. It's amazing what you can do when you have to. I stacked them all up using a combination of my good hand, good leg and a walking stick! And a mechanical grabber thing work mates thoughtfully bought me!

I kept at this for a few weeks. The nurses each day would think I was dropping them all the time or that I was just messy – which I am too! I just did whatever I could in-between the physio sessions. There were lots of things that could be improved in the hospital. I saw things that would improve morale, prevent infection, safety and patient recovery, some required money, but mostly they all had one thing in common, an inability to see things through the eyes of scared and vulnerable adults or of the staff. None of the changes would be expensive. In my 21 years in the NHS I've spent shifts on ambulances, in operating theatres, cleaning toilets and washing floors, as well as spending time talking with patients next to their beds. Until I became a patient. I realised I had never really seen it through their eyes. I was taught a valuable lesson about 15 years ago, regarding customer experience:

"That's all well and good, but do you have a daily feeling that you are going to be attacked or worse? No? Well I do."

I was wearing blacked out sunglasses and was undergoing equality training at a previous employer to try to better understand what it felt like for a blind person to visit our buildings. I was walking down a corridor then some stairs being accompanied by a colleague. Gently holding my arm, not taking my weight, just as a guide. When I returned back to the instructor who was blind, she explained to me that whilst I might be able to navigate a corridor and even some stairs with my eyesight completely obstructed by the glasses, But I would never feel the vulnerability that she feels when she hears footsteps or when she is out shopping and it is quiet in the street except for footsteps and then the sound of breathing behind her. She gets anxious and worries she is about to be attacked.

No pun intended; this really was an 'eye-opening' revelation to me. Sure I felt nervous, but I always knew I wasn't going to be allowed to fall down the stairs. As part of the training she explained that she is always in a constant state of heightened awareness and I thought that can't be good to have cortisol rushing through your body every time you go out. From then on, I cancelled the training and instead contracted this lady to undertake assessments of our building and help us to improve our experience rather than train staff members in darkened glasses. It's the same with colleagues asking me now about how I would improve acute stroke care.

Mine would be a completely different answer than if you had asked me whilst I was in a hospital bed, panicking that my family might leave me or I might lose my job, let alone never walk again. It's a whole different experience to looking back five years later from the comfort of my living room. I can't recreate that vulnerability at the moment.

The bedpan exercise came about out of utter frustration and disbelief. I made a note one day, in total over one day, excluding toilet trips, I spent 15 hours sat in a chair not doing anything whilst my muscles slowly atrophied – no physio came either. I knew it was no good for me. If a DVT didn't kill me, then the boredom would. I had to do something about it, so I devised the bedpan exercise to keep my mind occupied and at the same time help with my recovery.

I do want to express how great the staff are and how hard they work as a defence or some sort of balance, but that is never in question to me.

"You won't be able to get dressed like that with only hand Philip" said the therapist. "Especially your socks and shoes."

"No, what you mean is that YOU couldn't do it with one hand, you mustn't know me well enough yet, I'll do it!" I

67

told him, lifting my head up, looking into his eyes and smiling. He folded his arms and stood there watching like he was waiting for me to fail or struggle. I did it though, socks and shoes, both of them, and I still can. I even found a way to tie my shoelaces with one hand, thanks to a YouTube video I watched one night from my hospital bed on my phone, but that was more trouble than it is worth. I love trainer shoes, I almost collect them, so, I wasn't going to succumb to Velcro fasteners! It was another example of setting goals too low for me, I could do so much more. I was walking in my room alone, weeks before any of the staff knew. I trained myself, I had a few knocks and falls and I think a broken rib, but I accepted the risk. How much worse could it have been? I knew I'd do it, why would I tell anyone?

The hospital room I was in had one bed (mine) which was next to a very large window which was the length of the room, about 3 meters in length. Next to the bed, away from the window was a gap of about 3 meters with just a bedside cabinet and a moveable 'over the bed' table on casters. There was a comfortable chair and on the wall opposite to the window a sink. I was lying with my back to the window facing the sink, the doorway was on the sink wall at the other end. I tended to sleep with the 'nurse buzzer' close -to-hand, which was on a long cable next to me on the bed. The bed rails were raised as normal, but something had woken me and I could see through tired eyes a shadowy figure coming into my room and stand next to my bed about 1 meter away from me.

"Hello, who is that?" I muttered I was half asleep lying on my right side.

"Who is that?" someone replied. "It's me!" I said quietly, not trying to explain I was a patient. Sleepily in surprise, I realised it couldn't be a nurse as they knew who was in each bed. The shadowy figure carried on walking towards the sink not replying to me. "I'm going to the toilet," they eventually said. My eyes were becoming clearer now. I could see it was an elderly lady in her nightgown, about 80 years of age. I guessed because of her thinned out white hair which I could see from the moonlight coming through the broken window blinds on the opposite window. I pressed the nurse buzzer, but before the nurse could arrive, the lady had pulled up her nightgown and was sat on the sink having a wee! Thank god, she didn't need a poo!

"Philip, it is 1 AM in the morning, what is it that you want?" said a nurse standing in the doorway. "Sorry Nurse, but there's a lady sat on my sink having a wee, or I've just seen a ghost!" "Oh my god I'm so sorry… Joan! Joan! Come down off that sink, this isn't a toilet. Please come out of the room," said the nurse sternly, gently and a little nervous. Joan and the nurse left my room; I laughed. I still do at the memory.

"Helen, can't you control your patients? Joan had wandered into Philip's room," I could hear the nurses arguing between themselves outside of my room. The nurse came back to see me, she stepped in and pushed the door closed behind her. "Philip I'm really sorry about this, Joan can get a little confused."

"It's ok, please don't tell her off. I don't want to complain either, she has done no harm. And it's quite funny, but she hasn't washed her hands, nurse!" I said with a smile. "Also, would you mind cleaning down my sink and checking she has only had a wee!" the nurse smiled back, inspected the sink and then left the room. What a funny night. I went back to sleep quite easily afterwards.

"I woke with the sun streaming in through the gaps in the once white faded vertical blinds. I used the electric buttons to raise the back of my bed so I could sit up. I desperately needed a wee. I had the empty cardboard urine bottles stacked up next to me. I took one, and with my good hand held it to my penis. I was also wobbling a bit as my stomach muscles were weak and not 'firing' so I would lean to one side. Also, my left leg still wasn't moving above my knee, so it was a balancing act, holding the bottle to my penis. The bottle filled quickly and I was still going on.

As I took the bottle away, my bladder was weak and still is, my urine came out of the bottle and spilt upon my bed. I was sleeping on what's best described as a giant nappy, just in case I wet myself in the night. I placed the full urine bottle on the movable table next to my bed, the type of table on casters that goes over the bed when you want to eat. I pressed the nurse call buzzer for assistance a nurse student arrived.

"I'm really sorry nurse, I wet myself whilst using the urine bottle."

"That's okay," she said, "let me get some things to wash you and we'll get you sorted out in no time." She said that really cheerily and comfortingly. She made me smile and relax. I didn't feel embarrassed and realised this was just the situation I now found myself in. She was an excellent nurse, . You can tell the students apart as they wear white smart chef like tops with the University name embroidered on it. I've never understood it, but their uniforms were smarter than the qualified nurses.

She came back and, using a cloth, gently wiped me down and then dried me. The nurse got a clinical support worker to come and assist her to take me to the toilet. They placed me on the edge of the bed with my legs dangling over whilst they wheeled in what looked like a sack cart. The bed was lowered so that I could ease myself onto standing on the cart, which has a turntable on the base. I was then wheeled out of the room a bit like Hannibal Lecter, who was transported around his prison in the same way, but I had no face mask on, nor a straitjacket.

They helped me to the toilet. When I returned to the room, I was assisted back into bed. "There you are Philip, nice and clean with new sheets. There's no need to worry, it's what we're here for." I got a big beaming smile as the nurse said, "Would you like a cup of tea?" She clearly didn't know me very well! I always want a cup of tea!

"Yes please!" When she returned, she placed a cup of tea on my bedside movable table. It then all happened in slow motion. I could see what was going to happen, but the words just wouldn't come out. I couldn't move quick enough; the nurse pushed the table towards the bed so I could reach the cup of tea. She obviously thought the urine bottle was empty. The side of the bed got struck with the table, thump, the liquid in the urine bottle obviously moved and the weight transfer from the motion of the table tipped over the urine bottle.

The nurse had turned and was walking out the door, "Just call if you need anything else," she said cheerily and off she went and I was here once again in new pyjama trousers, new bedsheets and blanket but soaked in a container of my own wee!

"Yes Philip, can I help you?" said a very tall lady nurse I hadn't seen her before, but I am sure my blushing gave away what I had thought about her! "I'm really sorry nurse, I've just been changed after wetting myself but I dropped a full urine bottle on myself. I really am sorry for wasting your time…"

"It's not a waste of my time, I'm here to help you. Let me get some things to clean you up and we'll get you comfortable in the chair whilst we change the bed clothes for you." She came back and removed the bedsheets from underneath me, and then removed my trousers. It's funny my biggest worry in the hospital was having an erection at the wrong time, but it never happened thankfully. Not that there is a right time, just that I didn't want to embarrass any of the staff. "I've not seen you before," I said, making small talk whilst she washed me.

"No, I'm not always on this ward. I work on a temporary bank staffing rota. I'm a trainee doctor, but I like to do the clinical support worker jobs too so that I can build up my experience both as a doctor and as a caregiver."

I thought this was amazing and wondered why all trainee doctors do not do a stint as a support worker on a ward to help build up their understanding of relationships and communication skills. Maybe they all do, and I just don't realise? But she was the only one I met in my three months as an inpatient. I was helped by a nurse into yet another pair of pyjama pants and then helped to shuffle across the room to the large comfortable chair next to the bed, after she changed the bedding a nurse came into the room to assist me in getting dressed. I had a bag of mixed-up clothes next to the chair. I got out a pair of walking shorts and a T-shirt as well as my underwear. I dressed myself, I just needed help with things like fastenings and pulling T-shirts over my head.

I was dressed and sat in the chair now alone. Everybody else had left the room, the nurse had draped the nurse call button over the back of my chair, but I couldn't turn around enough to get it. I had a glass of water which had been left next to me on the now lowered table. After all this time I needed another wee. The constant need to use the toilet was a new sensation I was trying to get used to. After about two minutes of rocking the chair and bouncing it backwards and forwards as though it was a rocking chair, the buzzer bounced up and onto my left shoulder where I could now reach it with my right hand. You do become very resourceful when you need to, you pick up little tricks quickly.

I pressed the buzzer. Five minutes went by and I pressed it again, squeezing my muscles to stop from wetting myself. A nurse popped her head around the door, "I will be a minute, Philip, I just need to see to another patient first, okay?" I don't think it was a question as she left the room straightaway. "Nurse, I don't think I can wait, I need the toilet really quickly, please." I said in a loud voice hoping she heard me. She hadn't, as I suspected. She hadn't come straight back. 10 minutes passed and I couldn't wait any longer and I decided as I was now in pain and to let it out and wet myself.

The lesson to learn is never wet yourself whilst wearing walking shorts. They were waterproof and not only do they keep the rain out, but they keep the urine in! I had a small pond now growing in my shorts. There was obviously some soap powder remaining in the material of the shorts and underwear as soapy scented bubbles were coming out of my shorts. I sat back laughing at the scene; I thought it was hilarious. I'd become used to sitting wet; it was a fairly regular experience by now.

"Philip, are you okay?" Said Judy, the ward sister. I like Judy a lot, she was comfortable and kind to talk with.

I had made a friend in Judy, so I explained the whole story to her, and Judy quite rightly laughed with me. I was pleased she didn't try to be overly professional and not laugh; it's essential to be able to read people's feelings in her job.

I didn't wet myself again that day you will be pleased to know! But I'm laughing now as I write thinking about it! I call it my wee-wee story. It always breaks the ice at talks I deliver.

***

"Really? Vale is coming to see me?" I couldn't believe it. My dog was coming to the hospital to see me. This was like being told I could walk again. It was a fabulous feeling. It had been arranged by Judy, the ward Sister! I went on Twitter to say how excited I was. I was meeting him outside, Shana arrived and once I was helped into a wheelchair by Judy, Shana wheeled me out of the ward and into the elevator downstairs and then took me outside to the garden area at the rear of the building. Vale was quite a quiet dog, except when he was talking to me, of course. Shana went off to the car to get Vale. I waited patiently for a couple of minutes alone in the sun in my wheelchair. I was in the most awful hospital pyjamas; whoever chose them needs a sight check! they are bright orange and make you look like an inmate from Guantánamo Bay.

Woof, woof, came the voice, but I heard *Dad, Dad!* I craned my neck to the right and started crying. I could see my boy pulling at the end of his lead with Shana holding on tight. This is one of my most treasured memories of him. I loved seeing him and fussing over him. It hurt to see him go. He had an ear amputated whilst I was in the hospital due to cancer, and it was great to see it healing well.

I also enjoyed my kids visiting me, but I know they got bored coming in. My youngest was six at the time and was becoming a skilful gymnast. One time she had the nurses on

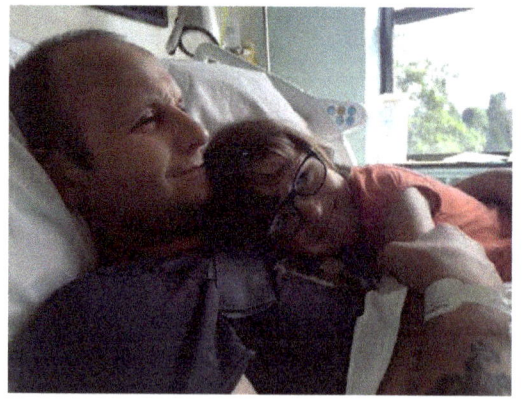 the floor of the ward with her, seeing who could hold a plank position the longest!

I returned home in mid-October 2016, and had learned how to stand and shuffle around with a walking stick. Most days, I would stand at the foot of the stairs in our hallway and slowly and carefully practice lifting my left leg up and down from the first step, concentrating on keeping my legs facing forward. Through the movement I would manage 30, before I became sleepy and unable to continue. I would then move to standing flat with my back against the hallway wall, my palms also flat against the wall. Then I would do 30 squats whilst keeping my back straight and chin up. My bum would be brushing the wall for balance as I went up and down. My penultimate exercise was hip thrusts lying on the bed, which was a mammoth task getting up the stairs. It went something like:

1) I would lie on my back on the bed with one knee bent and one leg crossed over the bent leg at the knee, my foot of the bent leg planted firmly flat on the bed.

2) I would press my heel into the bed, driving my hip upwards, pausing at the top, making sure to squeeze my glutes.

3) Slowly returning to the starting position and repeating after 10, I would then switch my legs, alternating until I couldn't do it anymore.

The therapists will tell you the bed is too soft for the exercise, but you have to improvise and it would be another few months before I was strong enough to develop a technique to get down and then back up from the floor.

My final 'exercise' I called temperature check. My left side of my body wasn't regulating its temperature very well, the temperature felt different on the left side (it still does).

I would get two bowls of water and use the kitchen tap to fill one with cold water the other with hot, not scalding water. I would then stand leaning against the kitchen counter for balance and practice mindfulness, concentrating on my breathing. I would then place my hands slowly into the water, each hand into a different bowl telling myself whilst controlling my breath which was hot and which was cold. I would end with my left hand going into the same bowl as my right – this exercise was to help my brain re-understand what was hot and what was cold, and it worked

I would test my improvement in my left arm – after 6 months at home (9 months post-stroke) it was still massively difficult to use it in a coordinated way. I could barely grasp or wiggle my fingers, yet the 'pasta game' as I named it, involved a bowl with dry pasta and two cup coasters. I would move one piece of pasta at a time to a coaster and each time, the aim was to put one more piece than before on each mat. I had variations of this exercise as my fingers regained more movement, involving coloured pasta; red went on one coaster, green on a green coaster and so on. These were the things I did to support my recovery. I tried electronic brain teaser games, but they made me tired and nauseous.

I also joined a local gym around the January after the Stroke. My carer would come with me too and help me with getting changed and showering, but I think it was really to keep an eye on me as the physio would get worried when I would climb onto a machine like the elliptical cross-trainer. But I was determined that I needed to build up my strength to cycle long distance firmly in my sights.

It took me about eight months, from being discharged to being able to walk without a walking stick. Leading up to that, I used to place chairs in a row across the dining room and kitchen using the backs of them to hold onto so I could get to the kettle and cooker, and back to the table to sit at and eat. I had bought a chopping board with spikes on to help me cut up food and butter bread as it held the food in place. Once movement returned in my left hand, I made a conscious effort to only use my left hand to open the kitchen cupboards. I would stand at a kitchen cupboard with a chair behind me so I could lean onto it, then I'd place my left hand with my right hand onto a kitchen cupboard draw handle, then open and close it 100 times with my left arm, or until it became

too painful to continue. At this time, my left shoulder was subluxated too. It was very sore and painful, affecting my sleep most days. I got back onto a bicycle about this time too. Pulling the front brake on the left-hand side was a challenge, but my friend's dad who works at the world-famous bicycle component maker HOPE, made me a device so the right hand brake lever could control both the front and rear hydraulic disc brakes! People are great! I would fall off quite frequently, but I didn't mind! And I insisted on still wearing cycling clip in shoes. My challenge was when I would stop quickly. My brain would get confused and try to put the wrong foot down and I'd topple over!

"Mum! Where's dad?" my youngest once shouted. My youngest was cycling in front of me along the canal side tow-path, Shana and my eldest daughter were ahead of us both. My youngest had stopped suddenly in front of me, and I was too close. I stopped and tried to put my left foot down as I was leaning to the left, but my brain stuck my right foot out. Over I went.

"I am over here in the bushes, help me out, please." I cried as my youngest tugged with two hands, pulling me up by my right hand as I reached out. I got to my feet scratched and a little bloody, but that just added to the drama!

I realised it wouldn't work safely. I'd either fall into the canal someday and drown or fall under a truck on the road. I sold all of my bikes and bought a three-wheel recumbent trike from a specialist manufacturer in Germany. It was a revelation. No more back or bum pain, and I could go quite far. I even rode 50 miles for charity through the night with my sister from Manchester to Blackpool Tower.

"Once I can ride again, I'll raise some money for the ward to say thank you," I told Judy the ward sister as I was discharged. And I did:

In 2017 less than one year after my Stroke, I toured the Netherlands on my trike with my sister Vicky and entered a mini-triathlon for the disabled called the Superhero series.

In 2017, I also walked across the Morecambe Bay sands as part of a guided walk, 10 miles in total, it was so tiring, but enjoyable too, especially as Vale and Shana were with me, I'm not sure how I did it as at times we had to wade waist-deep in water. But I did!

Last year (2020) just as the pandemic started, I stupidly ran 5k without any training in aid of the Stroke Association with my mate Dr Sarah Hart. I just did it; I knew in my mind I could overcome the pain, that it was not real. I told myself, drink plenty and control my breathing and take some Tramadol and I did it. Shana also jogged alongside me. It was nearly a year ago and I'm still in pain as a result, but we raised over £500 between us for The Stroke Association. I think I've really damaged myself from the run! Even Fentanyl no longer stops the pain. I can see that surgery might be needed. Apparently, a nerve has become compressed near the bottom of my spine.

I tried to scale the highest mountain peak in England in 2018, Scafell Pike but failed just over halfway. The fatigue and pain was awful. I lay on the grass in the sun and just wanted to sleep. But it was great fun, and I had lots of friends with me including physiotherapists from the Royal Lancaster Infirmary.

I have a goal and target, that by the time I'm 55, I intend to have walked to Everest Base Camp. If I find a way of raising £30,000 I'll have a crack at attempting the summit too if I can get my body into good shape. It's not a question of 'if' I will attempt it, but 'when' I will attempt it. I'm constantly planning it in my mind. Assembling the kit list, a walk through the mountain villages and seeing the Yaks carrying the loads with the Sherpas, I can't wait!

Chapter 4: Phil Is Dead, Long Live Phil

On August 6, 2016, I died and was reborn into who I am today. The old Phil whom I quite liked, was gone. The new Phil was different, and I'm sorry, that's just how it is. The new Phil is:

Slower; fatter, sadder; happier at times; just as creative; irritable; short-tempered; angry and tired and in more pain.

I struggle to describe whether I am tired or fatigued. I think it is the latter. I get exhausted, particularly if I have to read lots of documents or attend a meeting that requires concentration. Physical exercise makes me hungry and thirsty. I could go to sleep at any moment; on a park bench; in a gutter; anywhere. Noise wouldn't stop me, but sleeping doesn't make me feel any less tired, and the tiredness leads to irritability.

I have extreme mood swings ranging from high to low and bouts of creativity. I am also prone to act on things on a whim. Like deciding to write this book!

I used to get embarrassed over lots of things, particularly my body shape, but in this matter, something has changed in me. As part of a talk I give, I ask if people would like me to do the talk naked, bearing in mind I often deliver talks to over a hundred people at a time. Of course I am calling people's bluff, but it is my bluff to be called too! Literally, or is that buff?! I am serious when I make the offer. I don't say it because underneath my clothes, I have a six-pack and bulging muscles along with being well-endowed, all of which I want to show off; far from it. I say it is a practical demonstration of how my brain has changed.

I have also, I believe, become more caring and can see more beauty in things. This has led me to be more outspoken where I see unfairness or injustice. I really don't give a fuck, how much worse can it feel for me?

Less so now than the year after my stroke, but part of it is still with me. I'm happy to take risks as when you think you are dying, or you have been so depressed taking your own life seems like a less scary thing to do. "What is the worst that could happen?" I've asked myself in difficult situations. "I might get sacked, so what?"

I must be more careful with my own money as I have made mistakes, and I've never been particularly good at saving or making decisions to buy a low-cost item over a more expensive one.

I have developed strategies and techniques for most of these areas to help me cope, particularly at work. I have a good network of colleagues in my teams who, if I'm honest, keep me in a job – particularly a lady called Louise. I would have to leave my job if she ever left, as it would feel like I'd had my right arm cut off. I hope I tell her often enough what a great job she does. I'm sure she'll tell me if she ever reads this!

Chapter 5: Marriage

I wasn't happy in my job anymore, after transformation into the new Phil. I had lost confidence and needed to get it back. I wasn't as hungry or ambitious as I once was and where I could verbalise and explain my creative ideas. I was now struggling for words. I'd been back at work for a year since the stroke, and things were not going well between myself and my boss.

Shana and I had been talking about getting married for some time and wanted to help our children feel secure and started to set a date, etc. This all coincided with another event.

"Could we talk? My client is in Dubai and would be interested in talking to you." I receive a lot of job recruiter emails and phone messages throughout each year. This one arrived just at the right time on the right day when I was feeling particularly fed up. I replied, "Yes, I would be happy to talk." The exchange of phone conversations and emails went on for about three months.

The job recruiter was representing a financial investor who had bought hospitals in India and North Africa, and its head office for the Middle East and North Africa (MENA) region had been established in Dubai after spending billions of dollars! They were looking for an experienced hospital communications and marketing director. They had already recruited a chairman from the NHS, and their 'brief' was to continue to recruit in the NHS. There was a snag, and that was, we weren't married yet, and like it or not, we would need to be if we were to all go to Dubai, which was the intention, the salary was good. First-class airfares home four times a year and paid-for accommodation, and no tax of any note – what's not to like? The sun also shines every day.

My brother Chris was more or less working full-time in Dubai by then and his son, my nephew, had relocated there as a teacher. And I have another relative in Abu Dhabi working as a Nurse. It felt like a good move with people I knew already there. Not the most romantic of reasons, but we had spoken about marriage for a long time, and we agreed to continue with the marriage preparations and see what happens on the job front. (Shana, now seems to have forgotten all about the conversation!)

The job opportunity fell through at the last moment. I have my suspicions as to why, but they aren't mentioned in detail in this book. I think I would need to get a solicitor first. I had also applied for two other jobs in England, but despite a good first interview, the one I really wanted withdrew the opportunity and told me 'off the record' who had given me a less than favourable reference about me having the stroke and my abilities since – I know who you are. And I hope you sleep well at night? You thought I didn't know- well I did! I've learned that you tend to meet the same people on their 'way down' as you do on their way up, and this person now only has one way to go. So, I'm sure I will get the opportunity to return the favour at some point.

The second job I was offered but turned down, was in Leeds. I only told a select group of people about both opportunities, so it was easy to narrow down who said what as I hadn't told any of the same people about Leeds!

We still wanted to get married and were both very much looking forward to it. On a whim we agreed to get married abroad and have a holiday together with the kids too. In a day on my phone, I arranged a wedding planner in New York and via Air BNB, booked an apartment in the historic 'Hell's kitchen' area. My sister Vicky, and her friend Ruth, both flew out for the wedding and a holiday, as did Shana's mother, sister and brother-in-law Simon, who was also my best man. Two family friends who had known me since I was born, Maureen and Tommy also came along. They had moved to New York in the 1980s. It brought back great memories to see them both again; I've always loved them and their pretty daughters!

My mum couldn't make the trip, sadly she had just said goodbye to her husband Colin. He fought incredibly bravely after suffering a catastrophic stroke several years earlier. I loved Colin, he treated my mum really well. When I last saw him, I couldn't control my emotions. I held his hand and told him he was the only one that really knew how I was feeling.

The physical appearance was nothing I told him compared to the distress in my mind. Colin couldn't really speak any more due to the effects of severe Aphasia, but his smile and grip of my hand said it all. Goodbye, Colin and thank you, I will never forget you. Sleep well, my friend.

"Dad, you can't do anything normal, can you?" Moaned my eldest teenage daughter. "You didn't even have us both properly like other people (they were adopted)." "Where are you getting married?" She was in her bridesmaid's dress looking beautiful. We arrived at the banks of the Hudson River opposite Manhattan on an overcast April morning in 2018.

"Right here," I replied.

"Are you serious? We are on a street corner! People can see us. Why can't you get married in a church?" She proclaimed.

"Look at the skyline view and Manhattan Bridge. This is fantastic. Your mum is so happy being here; just make the most of it," I told her. She wasn't having it and stomped around. We decided we would all try to blend in and look a little hipster in New York. So, as well as wearing our wedding clothes, which was me in a suit, we were all wearing Chuck Taylor classic Converse trainers; me old school blue, and the girls all in pink Converse. It was an expensive way just to get some new shoes!

The ceremony took place with the officiate on the boardwalk right next to Manhattan Bridge at the beginning of Brooklyn. I didn't want to come home, some places when you visit they are great, but others are just a disappointment. New York, though, was bigger and better than I had imagined. I mean, sure, I knew it was a big city, but it was larger-than-life and I really liked the people living that way of life. Maybe one day. I'm not dead yet.

Chapter 6: Race

Race and ethnicity have impacted my life in different ways. I believe it had a positive impact on my views of others due to having a father who by birth was Malayan and certainly always saw himself as culturally Malay. This heavily influenced the food I ate and the conversations we would have. Dad grew up having an Armah, the acceptable name in his country for a maid and nanny. Dad always described his Armah as being black and in some way of lower standing and a servant.

As a child, a Sunday lunch out more likely than not would be in a Hong Kong Chinese café/Street hawker style restaurant in Liverpool's China Town. I'm sure we did eat in traditional pubs as a child. I just don't recall them. Dad loved to cook, his Curries were legendary, not so much for the incredible flavours, but more for the asbestos qualities your mouth needed! I can taste the crunch of curry puffs even today, a delightful mince and pea curry filling in what I assume was puff pastry. The flavours were intense and spicy against the soft, flaky pastry, a delight. We didn't have it often, but when we did, it was a real treat, along with his speciality of Chinese braised pig's feet in soy sauce. I've tried to find and recreate this dish several times over the years, the last time I threw it out onto the garden for my dog

Vale. The smell was horrible, and it was unbearable for Shana, all the more so since she was a vegetarian, I bet.

I am a huge believer in the impact of the sense of smell and our experiences. It is a scientific fact, not just a famed literary piece of work by Marcel Proust and his famous book, 'Remembrance of Things Past'. When your olfactory receptors are stimulated, they transmit impulses to your brain. This pathway is directly connected to your limbic system, the part of your brain that deals with emotions. That is why our reactions to smell are rarely neutral. We usually either like or dislike a smell. The smell of burning shrimp paste to this day takes me back to my youth. Belechan is a thick pungent paste that my dad used in his cooking, along with Lap Cheong Chinese sausage, especially in Fried Rice dishes or my favourite Indonesian rice dish: Nassi Goreng. Writing this evokes the smell in my brain and I'm smiling remembering the wok and smoking nut oil before the rice, egg and Lap Cheong are placed in along with the paste.

Wales is really is a beautiful country. I was scared of going to North Wales in the 70s. As a kid, I was aware from the TV of the arson attacks on English owned holiday homes. We had a caravan in North Wales. We'd regularly go especially if the weather was nice and on most school holidays, I'd sometimes be able to take a mate if my siblings were not coming with us.

"Hey coon, come here," dad shouted out of his van window. He thought this was perfectly acceptable and funny. I know I've embarrassed my kids, but this was a whole different level to anything I've ever since done. We were near *Colomendy.* The activity and education centre, Colomendy, will be a significant and evocative memory for many Liverpudlians who grew *up in the 70s and 80s as it was a regular school trip location in later high school years. I never got to go, but my brothers and sisters did.*

Dad had spotted a black man at the side of the road as we were driving to the caravan site just outside the town of Mold. The man was out walking on a lovely bright sunny Saturday summer morning. Up to this point, I was enjoying the journey in my cheap scratched mirrored sunglasses. Me and my mate went quiet, unsure what was happening. One of the reasons I liked going away with dad and a mate was that dad's temper was on 'best behaviour around other people'. It was a respite from his anger.

"Why did you do that, dad?" I asked. It wasn't so much the name that he called him with… This was the 1970s; black people, in my experience, were always called by a slang insult term. It was more that I didn't understand why he called the man over in the first place. "He wanted a cigarette," said dad. "Did he? How did you know that? Telepathy?" I thought to myself.

We must have been about 8. We were sat in the front passenger seats of the Ford Transit van. I thought I was the 'bees knees' with my mate upfront with me. I was wearing one of his Adidas three-stripe plain coloured T-shirts (now probably labelled as classics or originals).

I was very embarrassed about the word dad had called the man. I knew it was wrong to speak to people like that. How dare he? It just felt wrong, but in typical 1970s British style, we just laughed along, which I feel made me just as bad. My mate was called 'Stacey' and he took great stock in the fact that there was a famous American actor called Stacey Keech, mainly famous at the time for playing the fictional detective Mike Hammer from the Mickey Spillane books. I never remember Stacey taking any ribbing to any great extent from people about his name. He always stood his ground and gave as good as he got. I really looked up to him.

John, an elderly man, I'm guessing in his 80s, he'd been appointed a year earlier, as the Chairman of Morecambe Bay Hospitals where I now worked. John was a very experienced public leader and was once the first Chief Executive of West Lancashire Council. He was a jolly man, always smiling and welcoming. He had a good heart, and we got on very well. We would talk weekly, often at length on many subjects. I found he used me to try out ideas and bounce thoughts around. I could always be straight and honest with him. We both had that respect – I once had to 'talk' to him about his use of racist language.

He said the horrible phrase "N****r in the woodpile" in a meeting. I knew it was a 'slip of the tongue', but he deserved me to be honest with him. The meeting ended. people saw me go over to John and say quietly, "John can we have five minutes and a brew in my office when you have time today, please?" He nodded. It is a phrase I'm ashamed to say I'll have used hundreds of times before too, but that was decades ago when I did not know any better. It had been part of his vernacular, and I'd guess, along with P*k* to describe anyone of possibly Indian origin.

He used his age as a reason and excuse to me when I asked him to step into my office for a coffee and a chat. We'd become good friends since he had joined. He was intrigued that I grew up in Skelmersdale, where he was once a Chief Executive of the district council. I moved around from behind my desk to sit next to him and to be less formal. "You can't say that, John – it's not acceptable, ever." He knew before I even opened my mouth what was up. Still, his smile and body language, especially the shrug at my opening remarks, suggested that he didn't see it as that big a deal.

I shuffled uncomfortably, looking him in the eye and smiling, "I'm an old man, Philip," he said. I replied, "I don't give a fuck about your age, John. We are leaders and must set the tone and standard," I told him strongly. I know John didn't swear often. Swearing was deliberate on my part to 'raise the ante'. We shook hands and stayed in touch. He left the year later following a poor regulatory inspection. He kept in touch, sending me a lovely, heartfelt letter after he resigned. I expected no less than this, for him to take responsibility. He didn't look in the greatest health when I met him about two years ago in a local pub and gave him a present of the Bourbon 'Woodford reserve'. I do not take racism or bullying lightly. There's no grey area for me. You need to stamp it out even if it hurts people along the way as it's like cultural cancer if you let it persist, which is to accept and condone it, in my view.

A decade earlier, I had been 'asked to leave' the home ground of Liverpool FC, the football team I supported. A large group of men behind my wife and me were shouting and chanting racist comments at some of the black players whenever they were on our side of the pitch. I felt really uncomfortable. I looked around, surely others felt the same? Nobody else seemed to be bothered.

I caught the eye of a Black man sat on the other side of the aisle from me. He was sat with a child. We made eye contact, I mouthed 'sorry' and smiled. He looked away. Only 10 ft in front of me was a steward in front of an anti-racist sign, and he did nothing. I said to my wife! I'm not putting up with this." She told me to "calm down," I didn't.

I turned around to where the chanting was coming from. I told the group of lads to stop with their chanting. "You Black B*s****s," was still ringing out from their hate-filled mouths as I spoke. I was of course immediately threatened by them. "That's tough of you, I'm on my own with my wife and you are all lads together – I'm impressed," I responded sarcastically… and unwisely. I'm not too sensible when I lose my temper. I got up and walked to the steward who had witnessed this exchange and the chanting. I spoke to him, and I was asked to leave! I did shortly after.

The police had come into the section, spoke to the steward and stared me out, still doing nothing before asking me to leave the stadium. I expected to be arrested for some bollocks, like causing a disturbance. I wrote to the club after appearing on the local radio station phone-in show to air my views. The club wrote back and apologised for the steward and sent me two complimentary tickets for a match. But to add insult to injury, it was against Fulham, and with restricted viewing! I always felt my experience of Liverpool as a city, was terribly racist.

After my workmates heard me on the radio, a few of them said, "We heard you sticking up for N*****s" followed by the classic ignorant racist line of "We're not racist we have black friends too." I was godfather at the time to a black boy (CJ) so I took it serious that I must speak out.

I regret losing touch with CJ and his family, which is something I'm trying to correct.

"Joe is here." I cut my way through the cigarette smoke in the office and walked through the warehouse and opened the large roller shutter doors. Joe stood at the door, a tall man in his 40s, strong and stocky, wearing denim dungarees and steel toe capped boots and red PVC protective gloves. He unloaded the gas canisters he was delivering. We had a couple of coffees out of the cheap vending machine and had a laugh about the football. Joe wasn't happy in his job and was looking for a new one.

"Do they pay well?" He enquired.

"A driving job, Joe?"

He smiled and nodded, looking uncomfortable. This was the mid-1990s, around five years before the UK government introduced a national minimum wage.

"They don't pay great, Joe. About £4 an hour."

"Fuck me," he said in astonishment, "I get £8 now and that's with a HGV licence." I was looking at my shoes, waiting for the ground to swallow me up. Joe finished his drink, squashed the vending machine cup in his transformer Robot size hands and left.

"Joe is a good bloke, said a colleague," then there was a pause. I sort of knew what was coming, "for a black bloke that is," he added. One of my other colleagues came over from across the warehouse. "Yeah, he is good for a black man, but you're not thinking of offering him a job, are you? The lads wouldn't be happy, you know."

Now this is where I became complicit as I never said anything. I didn't stop the conversation. They already knew my views and that I didn't like this sort of talk. The discussion fizzled out with everybody looking uncomfortable around before all of us went back to our jobs.

The only people I knew growing up who weren't more or less the same colour as me was our GP and a boy in high school who had been born in Pakistan. Not to reinforce the stereotype, he was also the best cricketer in school, and his dad was also a local GP!

"Is now a bad time?"

I met Mr Patel in a corner shop/post office. He was mailing lots of parcels and I was buying my lunch – sandwiches and a bottle of Diet Coke. I caught up with him outside the shop, I explained what I did for a job (Parcel courier sales) and gave him my business card. He wore simple clothing, a white 'sheet' type of clothing covering most of his upper body and shoulders all the way down past his waist and to his knees. It was not really a dress, more like a blanket. It was wrapped around him, and according to Google, it appears to be called a Dhoti. Underneath a plain white shirt, he had no socks on, just a pair of brown brogues.

"A driver will collect my parcels every day?!" He said. He was clearly surprised, with a gentle melodic Indian voice and an accent I enjoy listening to. I agreed to visit him at his office the next day and talk him through the pricing and services. I was proud of myself for spotting the opportunity in such an unexpected place.

It turned out, when I arrived the next day, Mr Patel worked from home. He was a textile trader, and his parcels were samples he sent all around the world for his company based in India. I sat in his office with him, which was a room in the front of his sprawling bungalow, a bright White-fronted House and immaculately decorated and furnished. As we talked, he took off his shoes and crossed his legs. He then proceeded to cut his toenails! I found it amusing and accepted it as it didn't offend or bother me.

After an hour of discussion, we agreed on a discounted rate and daily collections of his parcels at 5pm. He was still sceptical that a driver would turn up every day without additional charge. I'd also thrown in a new desktop computer without charge, which would hold all of his customers' details and print his address labels and consignment paperwork for no extra money. I had several computers and printers in the back of my car – I always had several ready and set up to go. They will often be the deal breaker against my competitors at the time. I set it all up for him. He was overjoyed. This was a big account for the depot.

He spent around £2,000 a month sending his samples and the commission for me and the depot for international shipments was excellent. I was confident I would win the monthly national international sales award (again) if I got this account. I agreed I'd collect the paperwork the next week. It was a cutthroat business and did nothing to help my stress and anxiety. No wonder I developed psoriasis. I would attend a monthly regional sales meeting with all of my peers from across the North West of England.

The regional sales manager would discuss our individual performance; there were no private one to one discussions. Everything was done out in the open, and we knew at the end of the meeting if we still had a job or not. The pressure came if you hadn't hit your sales targets. There was a high chance you would be sacked when you returned to the office. I managed not to get sacked. The pressure was such that I always had what is called a healthy 'pipeline' of prospects lined up. Rather than go for the big prestigious accounts, I targeted lots of small ones instead. If I was parking my car and going to a sales appointment with a client, I made sure I called into every single business I passed on my way there or back. Even if that was 100 companies in an office block, I would knock on the door of every single one of them. Telling myself I only need one to say come in and I'd convert it as good as anyone else into business, I really was confident, be nice, polite, kind and explain the offering honestly and you'll be ok, I also understood something people still get really wrong in business and that is understanding the difference between a feature and benefit, mostly my competitors promoted the features whereas I knew how to convert them into benefits!

You could never miss an opportunity. You need to have tenacity and resilience as well as, I believe you need honesty to do well in sales. It's not the clichéd "gift of the gab" that a good salesperson needs. It's a good pair of shoes and ears. Do you know the biggest reason that salespeople don't close the deal? It is because they never actually ask for the business and they don't know when to shut the fuck up! I've witnessed sales people talk themselves out of 5-figure bonuses because they are not comfortable with silence.

"It was simple, Mr Patel, do we have a deal? A driver will turn up at 5pm every night, Monday to Friday and will deliver your parcels anywhere in the world for the prices on the special rate card. Shall I schedule the first collection on Monday or Tuesday next week?" There was then silence for about 10 minutes when neither of us spoke. Silence such as this can be deafening. I just sipped my cup of tea and smiled. Mr Patel did the same, until he broke the deadlock.

"Monday would be perfect," he said. Reaching out his hand to shake mine. As I shook his hand he put his other hand on top of mine. "This is going to be a good partnership," he said. It wasn't the money I just really liked him, and we obviously clicked. I placed my sales presenter – which was a desktop flipchart into my briefcase. These were the days before affordable laptop computers. I walked back to my car with a spring in my step. As I sat in the car, my right leg felt funny. I reached down, my calf was itchy. I felt a mound of flaky skin and picked at it. A piece of skin flaked off my leg about an inch long and a few millimetres thick. This was the start of my psoriasis.

I wasn't well with an upset stomach (polite way of saying I had diarrhea/the shits) and it took a couple of weeks for me to get back to Mr Patel's house. I arrived without an appointment. The driveway was a semi-circle with gates at either end, but it was full of large black Mercedes cars, and the road outside had no parking spaces. I parked about 5 minutes away, grabbed my Antler, black leather briefcase and a small gift I'd bought Mr Patel to say thank you. I'd been into Preston and bought him an ornamental Taj Mahal desk tidy with a letter opener. I always bought new customers, regardless of the account size, a present out of my own money to say thank you.

A lady answered the door. She was wearing a plain white, but beautiful Sari. "Is Mr Patel available please?"

"I'm sorry he's gone," said the lady.

"Gone?" I replied confused. The lady responded softly but stuttered, "I'm his w…w…wife," and she said he had died. "It's his funeral today."

I gulped and felt my palms get sweaty. I felt hot under my shirt collar, "I'm really sorry to hear that. He was a lovely man. I had a gift for Mr Patel, may I give it to you?" I handed the gift-wrapped package over.

"If it's not a bad time, did he leave a document for me?" His wife said her son was taking over the business, but he was busy today. "If it's not a good time, I can come back," I couldn't believe what I had just said – of course it wasn't a good time! Mrs Patel took me to her dead husband's office.

"Please help yourself and see if you can find what you're looking for!" I nervously looked on the desk. I found the folder I had left Mr Patel with all the documents. Inside was the completed and signed account paperwork – I had taken a risk letting him trade without first completing the account application form. I took the form and left my business card with a note on the reverse for her son to call me. It turned out to be a great account. I bought a brand-new Tag-Huer watch with my first month's commission. I still have it, but it is in need of a bit of TLC sentimental value for me now and replaced by a not so smartwatch that appears to spend all day telling me I don't move enough!

I was saddened he'd died. We had hit off, and I thought I'd met someone who would become a good friend in time. I loved his obvious eccentricity.

In one way or another, different races and colour have been instrumental in my life at different points. I'm proud to say in 35 years of recruiting and appointing people, I've never NOT appointed a BME person I've interviewed. I would not appoint if I thought they would be a danger to anybody in terms of capability, but in my opinion, it is the difference between equality and equity and helping to create opportunities for people who need it.

A transient ischaemic attack (TIA) or "mini stroke" is caused by a temporary disruption in the blood supply to part of the brain.

The disruption in blood supply results in a lack of oxygen to the brain.

Chapter 7: How Open Am I Being? And Growing Up

I won't be 'naming names' where I don't have to, and I  won't be listing my sexual exploits, there aren't that many! I don't believe these sorts of memories are mine alone; there is always another side to a story. I've been as brutally honest as I can be and have taken responsibility for my actions. Of course, I will have kept some skeletons still firmly locked in the closet. You don't get to be 50 years old and climbing the job ladder without pissing off a few people along the way, rightly or wrongly!

I was a bad husband the first time around. I know it takes two to make a relationship work, but I do believe I was the reason it ended. Kate, my first wife, is a good person, now living a good life with a nice man and children in another country, according to her social media! I miss her at times. I don't believe you can share so much with another person and not still have feelings of some sort. It's not love in a desirable sense, but I still feel a connection and wish her no harm.

We met when I was 20 and a delivery driver. My mate Neil was dating Kate's friend Lorraine. We met on a blind date, in a club/pub in Wigan called 'The Underground'. I was an hour late too! I'd been working in London all day, delivering computer tapes to secure data vaults and the drive back on a Friday up the M1, and then the M6 was as torturous as I'd ever encountered. Nine hours non-stop, I was shattered and had to get changed and cleaned in my van outside the club! I came into the club nervously and went straight to the toilets where I had a wash in the sink, stuffed some mint chewing gum into my mouth, a bit of deodorant for my body, and then went to the bar.

Neil gave me a huge hug. I felt like throwing up with nerves. He looked as cool as a cucumber as always, blonde, jaw-length hair and Stone Roses T-shirt underneath a plain untucked open shirt. I asked the girls what they wanted to drink and bought them doubles! Malibu and Coke. Kate and I hit it off straight away.

The Underground was a bit of a dive. It was essentially in a cellar of a pub, dark and noisy with flashing lights and the tables were upturned barrels with highchairs. We stayed for a couple of hours and then headed over to a nightclub, 'The Wigan Pier'. It was more a disco than a true nightclub, located on the Canal side and hugely popular playing host to the 80s late night TV show The 'Hit Man and Her' on Occasion featuring Pete Waterman and Michaela Strachan. Coincidentally, I'm actually friends today with one of the male dancers from the show.

We met regularly over the coming weeks before she explained that she was immigrating with her parents to Vancouver, Canada, in a few months. Her mum and dad had been unsuccessfully trying to emigrate for the best part of a decade but had just then been successfully accepted, and their house had been sold too! Kate had just turned 17 and was studying for her A levels at a college. I was devastated that she was leaving, especially after having finally met someone I found impeccable chemistry with. It was to end, which kept becoming more difficult as I got to know her more and got along really well with her brother, Mike, her parents Eddie and Joan. I felt like I had found a new family and enjoyed my time going round there. Eddie even had a Motorbike!

I was a fat kid, not chubby, or 'puppy fat', whatever the hell that is? I was fat, plain and simple. Now, there are lots of fat kids, it is sadly accepted, but in the 70s and early 80s, McDonald's hadn't yet erupted in the UK. I was the exception at school, always picked last for sports, and nobody wanted to sit next to the fat kid, especially the girls. Kentucky Fried Chicken (KFC) was a huge treat as there was only one shop, and it was 30 miles away.

I used to love the scented hand wipe that came with it and covered in chicken grease in the box! I would be sat in the back seat of our Datsun estate car waiting for the treat, chips in a paper bag inside a box, with two pieces of grease-laden crunchy spiced chicken breast nestled next to them. The car would smell of food for days. I've never liked eating with my fingers much, the grease of the chicken would stick to my fingers and the hand wipe which you were given was in a foil wrapper, a bit like a condom wrapper and difficult to open with greasy hands. Still, once you got the wet tissue delight out of the wrapper, you could then wipe your mouth and fingers before drying them with a paper napkin.

I really do hate KFC now. It is one of those foods that I sometimes crave, but it is more the thought for me of the food. I find it disappointing once I taste it, the wonderful hot smell of the mystery blend of herbs and spices takes me back to a nice place in time, but when I do eat it, I tend to feel bloated, guilty and then usually a bit nauseous. I remember ordering KFC in Malaya near the Sepang Race Circuit. My Bother Chris and I had spent the day watching pre-season testing as Valentino Rossi tried out the new M1 Yamaha. We had the whole stadium seated area to ourselves! Anyway back to KFC, Chris waited in the hire car – the chicken was raw when we bit into it, but it was worse than that, there was no lemon-scented hand wipe. I marched back in and dumped the half-eaten chicken on the counter trying to explain it was raw and there was no scented hand wipe in a wrapper! I know, no hand wipe! Forget the potential of botulism!

I was active as a kid; a 'latch key kid'. I came and went mostly as I wanted. The reason I became fat was due to a combination of poor diet and long periods of feeling sad and comfort eating when I was young. There were a few things I wanted to be when I grew up: vet – it didn't take long to realise I wasn't clever enough for that; secondly – a chef, which was my dad's influence. I was never pushed into any area, but he was always cooking and I learned plenty of tips from him. And third, I wanted to be my elder brother, Chris! I've never told him this, and although we had scraps, he was always someone I looked up to. When he joined the army, I used to brag to all of my mates about it. I would get so excited when he'd come home on leave.

One year, my brother brought me a tank helmet home with a microphone and built-in sliding sun shield. It was probably the best present I had ever had. I say present, but typical big brother, it wasn't a present; he had to take it back with him when he returned from leave. His kit bag and uniform seemed really exciting to me. The kit bag always smelt musty; I would imagine that he would carry supplies in it as he crawled through the undergrowth into battle! I loved and still love all my brothers and sisters like that. I don't tell them often enough though.

Growing up. Mum and dad would argue a lot, or to put it more accurately, dad would shout. I don't mean they had a few raised words, I mean they'd be really shouting. I'd sit outside our living room or in my bedroom shaking and crying, listening intently for the tell-tale signs that there was a lull in proceedings as it tended to follow a pattern. Occasionally, there would be a calmness and mum might appear to make a brew or get more cigarettes or tell me it would be all okay. I needed and miss that reassurance; something that is still dominant in my life is seeking and needing reassurance when I feel vulnerable, but don't we all?

Social media is something I am wrestling with at the moment, I'm seriously considering deleting it entirely from my life. This will be a challenge as it has become a big part of my occupation and virtual persona too. Still, I feel it is largely a narcissistic practice and unhealthy, not exactly the amount of time people spend on it that's unhealthy, rather the feelings and emotions it stirs up in others and me. Like most regular Social Media users, I enjoy that feeling of receiving a digital applause. The 'like phenomenon' – a Harvard Researcher[1] reports that this sensation is actually a rush of dopamine to the brain. This can't be healthy, what if I spent the same amount of Social Media time on exercise or reading?

1 https://sitn.hms.harvard.edu/flash/2018/dopamine-smartphones-battle-time/

I realised years ago; dad was, I believe, a mentally ill man. He would wake me up, and I think the rest of the family, sometimes as early as 4am, usually by banging things such as plates in the kitchen sink, slamming doors or banging the kitchen chairs as he moved them. He also played loud music, not thrash metal, but the Carpenters or maybe Dr Hook. Maybe this was his 1970s dopamine satisfaction kick?

This part certainly dates me! So, let's get it over with. I am soon to turn 51, and I was born in 1970. It was usually the Carpenters, or on some other occasions, the sounds of Crystal Gale that would fill the house, or Dave Brubeck and Take 5 – I really couldn't care less about 'Rainy Mondays' or 'Sylvias Mother', I just wanted to sleep. Dad would sometimes come into my bedroom muttering some shit 'till you had to argue back with him. I would pull the blankets up over my head, pretending to be asleep, pulling my knees up to my chest into the foetal position, which felt safe and reassuring. I could hear footsteps across the bedroom until he would be next to me. He would sometimes tell me problems before going into a further rage.

One morning around 1979, he sat down next to me on the bed and held my hand as he lay down next to me. He was in his Y-Front underpants and vest and fell asleep snoring. I put one arm across his chest. I could feel his chest rising and falling. I rubbed my forehead against the stubble of his chin, which felt strangely reassuring. This attention I was showing was keeping him quiet, so I thought I would play along with it. He opened his eyes as he snored, and whilst holding my hand gripped it tighter, he turned his head and looked at me.

"Philip, I'm dying."

His eyes were wide now. Not teary, but they looked emotional, like I could see right into his soul through them. I truly did dislike him, maybe even hated him at this time in my life, but his words that day worried me like it would any child who would hear their parent say these things. He was still my dad, and largely, he was the one that put food on the table. My thoughts were scrambled. What would we do if he died? I thought. Should I go and get mum? Is he dying right now?

"I don't understand, dad, right now? Or later?" I questioned. He laughed a little bit whilst I was thinking, then said, "It's just the back pain, Philip. I can't take much more, it is 'killing' me, and I will soon die." He also suffered from ankylosing spondylitis, something I now know can be inherited and can run in families. I can fully understand the pain he must have been in. I sometimes have to stop when I'm walking up the stairs at home or at work to catch my breath because of the searing pain running through part of my spine. But even so, I wouldn't go so far as to be this dramatic. But I do now fully appreciate the despondency he was feeling. The fatigue and depression that can often come with it.

I hesitate telling people how much the pain I go through impacts me as it can be very invisible, and the reply tends to be, "Yes, I have a bad back too." "No, this isn't because I'm lazy and fat, you arsehole." I want to yell back, "I'm walking or cycling today." I want to tell people because the Fentanyl doesn't help anymore, only keeping active does, and although the exercise hurts, it means I might sleep tonight! It's my dream to have a house large enough to create a gym so I can keep active all day, and if needs be, even work in it!

Anyway, so after that, Dad eventually sat up and got out of my bed and went downstairs, leaving me to wonder when is he going to die, later today, and tomorrow? I was confused, I'm sure I've said this, but I do often take things very literally.

"Won't you stop and take, a little time out with me?" Sang Dave Brubeck out of the hi-fi speakers. Dad was awake, this meant the whole house now had to be awake too. It would leave me wondering, how were the police never called by our neighbours? Or maybe they were, and I just didn't know about it?

Until the age of 18, I spent most of my time 'on edge', waiting for him to 'start'. It would feel like being perched constantly on the edge of the seat. My legs would involuntarily twitch and move. I worried not just about the day I was living in, but also about what was going to happen the next day and most of all at the weekend. I wrongly blamed mum for a while, asking myself when he lost his temper, why would Mum say that to him. It's obvious he'll lose his temper now. I feel sick thinking that I blamed her. She was a victim and I didn't realise it as a child. I know my dad hated my mum having opinions; he held a very outdated and chauvinistic view of women and their role in a marriage. I now know my thoughts were wrong. It's akin to blaming a woman for being attacked because her skirt was too low. She should be able to be naked and not get attacked; these are basic human rights. Victims are called victims for a good reason; they are not to blame; they are the victim.

My feelings at the time would now be labelled as stress or anxiety. I can't believe the GP never spotted any pattern of my weight gain, not once as a fat kid, and by fat; I mean very fat! My GP never offered any advice or suggestions as to how I might lose this killer growing around my body and organs. The constant upset stomachs were treated with some pill or another and a day off from school. Medicine and science have advanced massively since I was a boy, but I feel what has changed massively is attitudes. Sadly as a country, we've accepted the label of being the 'fat man of Europe'.

My health conditions today can now be primarily predicted and prevented early on. Ankylosing Spondylitis, for example: clinics can now test for a particular gene known as HLA-B 27. Having the gene does not necessarily mean you'll develop the condition, as it is estimated that eight in every 100 people in the general population have the gene, but most do not have the condition. So it is not the most reliable of predictors. However, having the gene can make you more vulnerable if tests show that you have the gene. This raises the chance you could pass it on to any children that you have.

Was this available when I was growing up? I will probably never know, but if it was, it was a missed opportunity along with identifying the signs of stress and anxiety with long periods of missing school through illness of some sort or another, then in later years just not going to school. I'm convinced there were enough clues to show signs of an unhappy child, but maybe that's easy to say from where I view it from?

After the morning's impromptu concert, dad would often let loose with his temper. I can't speak for my siblings as they appear to think the sun shined out of his backside and to have adjusted well. They don't seem to view this behaviour as abhorrent as I did and still do. Me, I wanted to hurt him, I hated him for how he would treat mum, all of us. I just assumed this is how all children were treated. I'd regularly feel the thunder of his hands on my backside. Then his leather belt as he stood over me sweating and panting in his saggy Y-fronts and vest stinking of cheap stale Lambert and Butler cigarettes and sweat – that's probably why I've never smoked. The stinging on my backside would be unbearable. I did all I could to hide the pain.

Once all I had done was take a pen from his desk to use to draw with, but this was stealing in his view. He had now escalated to a bamboo cane, the type used in a pot plant. *Thwack!* it landed on my bare fat backside, springing back with each stroke. Remarkably I could always take the pain and never begged for it to stop. I wasn't going to give the bastard the satisfaction, but I certainly did cry with snot dripping out in my nostrils onto the carpet. Was this what all dads did or was this how he was brought up by his father and Armah? I guess I will never know, and I certainly never asked him. I saw the brass letter opener sat on his desk and for a moment thought of reaching over to it and driving it into his chest such was my hatred and anger that day, I'm breathing faster just writing about the feeling and memory.

In part, I have chosen adoption as a way to start my family so that my father's genes were not passed on, and I was scared I had the bad ones in me. On occasion, I can feel myself wanting to act like him, and at times it makes me feel sick to feel that way. I have a short fuse and a bad temper, which I have always had – but heightened since the stroke, as though the stroke 'turned the short fuse dial' up a notch or two. Only my wife and kids can tell their view of me, I can't do that for them, but I'd take my life if I thought I was a danger to them. My youngest tonight said she was angry with me, and that I was nicer before I had a stroke. This really hurts and I must try harder.

Since the stroke, I've definitely changed, and it is frightening to me. I can control it to a point. Situations outside of the home where I've felt the feelings grow, I could really end up doing some serious harm to somebody, including myself. We've a new rule at home for when I can't control myself. The 'rage' I feel boiling up inside, it is like a thermometer. I can literally feel the heat rising through my body, and my breathing changes. I hold both of my hands up, and everyone gives me space to go and sit quietly and calm down while everybody stops talking.

It makes me so sad to think about what happened only a few days ago. My youngest at 11 helped me. She stopped everyone from talking in the Kitchen when I raised my hands, and she was very strict with the family to leave me alone. I haven't slept properly since thinking about it. Have I turned her into the 11 year old me, scared of her dad? Or is it just her being her usual kind self? This isn't the life I wanted for them; they shouldn't have to do this.

I can remember my father collapsing at his workplace when I was relatively young, perhaps 9 or 10. He was taken to the hospital in an ambulance. I remember pretty clearly standing and holding Mum's hand in the hospital and confused that "Why she was so upset?" Sure, show a bit of sadness, mum, I told myself, so he didn't get angry, but not too much.

"Mrs Woodford," said the doctor, "we've done all the tests, but we just can't find anything wrong with him," explained the doctor, I looked up at mum, she looked worried and puzzled and told me it would all be okay. Mums are great at knowing what to say at such times. She looked so tall and alone in the hospital we were stood at the end of a ward – they would now be called 'Nightingale wards', a bit like in the carry-on films; it was just one large room/ward. Now I wonder if he'd had a TiA or something similar, we'll never know.

In the middle of the ward was a desk with nurses sat at it. We were stood at the entrance around the room there were men in beds, all looking poorly and in their pyjamas, curtains were pulled around some of the beds. I couldn't see dad. He was in a side room. Looking back, it seems he had a breakdown with the stress of his work. Dad never went back to the same job, instead he started his own transport company OTEC (On Time Express Couriers), initially from a bedroom in the house before renting his own premises.

I would sometimes be taken to the pub with dad. I don't ever recall having a 'babysitter'. I was a child who wouldn't stay with other people. Therefore, I was always taken wherever my mum and dad went. I would describe myself as a mummy's boy. I'd sit quietly in the corner in the pub listening in. I hated and still do the vile cigarette smoke. It would hurt my lungs and nostrils. The air was pungent and foggy. Boredom would set in pretty quickly, and I would daydream. Usually, I would be flying a fighter jet off into war until laughter broke out or one of the other men would recognise the boredom and tried to help me by engaging in a conversation. I remember one of the pubs being the Hill foot Arms in Speke, Liverpool, sitting in the snug.

The snug was an area of an old pub, usually an alcove or smaller room, sometimes with a serving hatch and was an area affording some privacy from the rest of the pub. Some of them were better than others and would have a dartboard or pool table in it. I had my own set of darts; I was no expert at it, but I could play well enough that the other men would entertain me by playing a 'round' of darts, usually a game of '360' or '240', where the aim was that the winner was the first person to score either 360 or 240 depending on which game we were playing. I would usually drink a bottle of Coca-Cola and eat peanuts or pork scratchings – no wonder I've had a stroke! I'm amazed I got to 45 without it happening earlier. At the same time, dad got drunk, smoked and talked business.

One day in a pub, shortly after he had been discharged from hospital, the conversation was different. "Terry, has a plan to shoot him," said one of the men as they puffed on their smoking pipes. I did like pipe and cigar smell; if it's the right tobacco, I still would. This sentence had made me land my spitfire and listen more intently. "He can't put up with Dennis any longer, it nearly killed you, Pat (Patrick was my dad's name)." Dad just nodded. They were talking about one of their work colleagues who was planning to shoot their boss, Dennis. Dennis was a rich man, a bit like Arthur Daley from the 1980s British sitcom Minder, sheepskin jacket and all, including the minder! He had greased black hair, greying as I recall. I even had a 'minder' once, long story, but I received some threats when I was successful at winning some new business from a competitor, my bosses at the time paid for a man to spend the day with me in my car when I was working in case of trouble, he was a great bloke, 'massive' and menacing with a big soft heart! 'Big John' everyone called him.

I remember visiting Dennis's house on the Wirral with dad. We pulled up in dad's Datsun (pre the Nissan brand name) behind the 1980s archetype villain's car, a gleaming maroon 1970s Daimler Sovereign, with plush cream leather seats. It was a beautiful car in the days before alloy wheels; lots of chrome glinting in the sunlight, especially the hub caps. The tyres of dad's car crunched on the long gravel-covered driveway. I had never visited a house this big before. It had impressive concrete pillars on either side of the front door. I thought I was in Rome visiting the Coliseum! Dennis came around from the side of the house and shook hands with dad.

"Hi Philip," he bellowed in what is best known as a "plastic scouser, semi-posh voice". We followed Dennis around in through what looked like an orangery, but I would call it a large wooden lean-to conservatory. We walked behind Dennis into an equally large and expensive-looking kitchen. The house was cold and very quiet, the countertops were made of marble, a grey and white affect. I had never seen a marble kitchen countertop before, only laminates with bits hanging off the edges, and dried glue. I was careful not to touch anything with my mum's voice running through my head of, "Don't break anything, Philip," which is what I was always told whenever we went into a shop with breakables in it.

"If you break it you have to pay for it." It was one of those silly things that parents say… I mean how the hell would a child be able to pay for breaking wine glasses in John Lewis? It's nearly as daft as my mum's favourite question, "Do you want a smack?" "Yes Mum, I'd love nothing better than a bloody good smack, thank you!" But of course, that response would likely get me the belt across my backside for being cheeky.

Back to the kitchen now. I had never seen a cooker in the middle before. The extractor over it really was one fit for a Michelin star chef. I thought I could smell some familiar food. "Here Philip, have a glass of water," said Dennis. I was a bit shocked. All this money and he only had tap water? I was hoping for dandelion and burdock, my favourite pop. I heard the front door close, and I don't know why but my heart raced a little bit, in anticipation. I heard footsteps from the front door, then down the hallway, heavy steps on the immaculate parquet flooring. A man in a black leather jacket with long hair came into the kitchen carrying a cardboard box. I instantly recognised the smell, chips! "John, put the box on the countertop, please," instructed Dennis. He said it in such a way that the please felt like it was for our benefit as the guests rather than out of politeness. John did as he was asked. Dad was pouring himself a whiskey and one for Denis too.

"Let me square up the bill with you, John, I owe you for last night too," Dennis took out a bundle of money from inside his jacket. "It is okay, Dennis. We can settle it tomorrow when I collect you." Dennis just nodded, and John turned and left the house. John had the most immaculate shiny shoes I had ever seen. I could see the reflection of the kitchen lights in his shoes. "I'm sorry gentleman," Dennis said to us both – gentlemen! I giggled at being called this, and dad clipped me around the ears and quietly said, "Manners!" I knew to shut up and only speak when you are spoken to.

I knew my place and promptly shut up, losing my customary grin. "Maureen is away visiting her mother, so I'm afraid nothing has been cooked for your visit. But not to worry we have the best fish and chip restaurant in the whole of England." Really? I thought to myself, what a stroke of luck that is that the best fish and chips in the whole country are made right here near Dennis's house.

Dennis dished out a portion of fish and chips for us each onto large white plates with gold and blue flowers around the edges. There were tall chairs like I had seen in the pubs in the kitchen and we all sat on one and ate our food at the kitchen counter. They were nice, but I thought as I ate them, yes they are nice but they are no different from the chips we get at the shopping parade. "Dennis, thank you for the chips. They are lovely and the fish is the best I've ever had," I lied. I could feel my tummy grumbling under the weight of the oil and batter of the fish.

We didn't stay much longer, and as dad backed out of the drive, he said, "He has always been a tight Bastard, all that money and bloody chips for tea. No wonder he's rich." He said this in an unusual tone that suggested not so much jealousy but anger and frustration. There was a scraping sound as dad reversed the side of the car into the gate bollards! Dad didn't stop though, he carried on and the driver's side chromed wing mirror fell off as he went. Dennis was stood at the top of the drive, watching and waving. He

127

must have seen what had happened but didn't come over or said anything. He just stood there with one hand in his pocket and the other waving at us.

I'm not aware that Dennis was ever killed. After that night, I never really heard his name mentioned again until several years later when dad's business was doing okay and he had employed a full-time sales manager, a man called Wally. Wally, it turned out used to be the salesperson for Dennis's business, and dad had received some threats for taking business away from Dennis.

Chapter 8: How Well Do You Know Anybody?

 Dad was getting much older now. I had fallen out with him for many years, about 10. Both Chris and Vicky agreed that they would take him to Malaya for a possible final trip home. I agreed that I would come along too as it would be nice to get to know him and maybe he would be different there.

We were sat on a street corner outside a local café. It was a cobbled street in the historical and old town of Malacca where dad had been born some 75 years ago. It was a rickety plastic green garden with table and chairs, certainly not a five-star dining. The waiter was a very tall slim young man with a dirty food stain on what was once a white apron covering his clothes. He came to take the order. We had all been pulling dad's leg that he wasn't really from Malaya and couldn't speak the language, so he ordered our meals in Malay but the waiter didn't understand him and had to explain he wasn't Malaysian himself. Could we order in English or Japanese, he requested. "Yes I will order in

Japanese," said dad, still blushing with embarrassment from the earlier attempts and the leg-pulling he received from Chris and me, and off he went ordering for meals in fluent Japanese. It must have been 60+ years since he had had to speak the language.

"How do you know Japanese dad?" I asked perplexed. "You forget your history Philip, Malaya was an occupied country during the Second World War, and we all had to learn Japanese at school. "Okay, I understand that, but we all had to learn French at school and none of us can speak it, how come you can speak Japanese still?" I challenged. "Because we spoke it every day as conversations with the Japanese. It is hard to forget something you did every day for many years." He made a good point, we were all really impressed, and it deserved more beer and piss taking. He took it all in good humour, and I started to see a different side to him. He was really relaxed without the stresses of home life. I found it hard to see this other side of him, the caring, relaxed and attentive dad. You think you know somebody, but really how well do we know anybody?

"I bloody love humans..." said David Tennant, as Dr Who, and I can relate. I just love people and our differences I think it is amazing. "I'm a commercial pilot..." "I speak fluent Russian..." "I used to be in the air force..." These were the different answers from members of one of my team recently when I asked them all to tell me something about them that I couldn't guess.

For two years, I sat in an office next to one of them every day. Only turns out that she has been a trained commercial air pilot all along. I wasn't shocked that she had the calibre and ability to be a pilot, it just reminded me of the importance of not taking people for granted. I've seen it lots over the years in the NHS. When the NHS comes across a problem, it brings in the expensive management consultants, it really is a waste of money. With 7000 colleagues where I work, many of them have run their own businesses successfully and had more experiences in life that many of us could only dream of. I've realised to my cost over the years the answers to most problems and issues are closer than you think if you have got the courage that is to trust people who don't have the elevated title. These instead might be the people who push the broom past your office every day.

Take the time to get to know them, please. Leaders who treat people like they are stupid, should expect stupid behaviour in return. I was massively depressed as an inpatient; I would lie to the doctor and nurses about how I felt. I didn't want to believe I couldn't cope or that I needed any help. I'm Phil Woodford, I can get through this blip, but the only person who really knew my mood other than me, was David, The Ward Cleaner! He saw and spoke to me every day, and I'm talking about proper conversations about interests and experiences. But when I attended the meeting (MDT) where all the different specialists come together to discuss a patient's progress, he was not there, neither was the first person to see me every day for nearly 4 months, the volunteer lady who brought the morning tea and newspaper. A very big, missed opportunity in my opinion – what do you think?

I work with some fabulous people who possess incredible talent and intellect. As surgeons they cut people open for the living, which an incredible responsibility, yet many of them don't have the authority of responsibility to make purchasing decisions. We trust them with the most precious thing, people's lives, but we employ a raft of managers above them to make the 'difficult 'decision of spending a mere £1000 or more. It's not just where I work, it's the whole of the NHS. I do dream of being in a more senior position as I would like to have the authority to take the shackles off people, particularly doctors and nurses and let them 'run' with the decisions. I have every faith that they will do the right thing. Sure there will be mistakes, but who doesn't make them? When your child is dying and needs an operation, it won't be a manager like me who diagnoses, cares and treats them. Who is it you would rather have design, purchase and arrange for the equipment and environment you or your loved ones are cared for in? The person you put your child's life in the hands of, or the stranger in a suit like me? It's the former for me, and I've been there for real with my kids.

Chapter 9: A New Beginning

Good on her, Mum left dad when I was about 11 or 12. I don't know if she had met someone else. I hope she had as she deserved better. Mum ended up starting her life again, first in the seaside town of Southport in Merseyside.

I have a tormenting memory. I think it was the day after mum left. I was crying a lot (I did as a kid!). I was allowed to stay off school for a day. I went out on my BMX to clear my head, it was a 80s icon – a Raleigh Burner. I'm 50, and I still think about buying another, I do love bikes – my dream job would be a city cycling mayor, or to own a bike shop even in the internet shopping age. I rode to visit a family friend and talk; Anne and Jimmy lived about a mile away across the housing estates. With tears and snot dripping from my face, I knocked on the door. Skim, for all its faults, was easy to navigate away from the roads. I would like my kids to experience that freedom of roaming with no worries of cars and trucks. When I arrived at Anne and Jimmy's house, I wasn't prepared for mum answering, nor was I prepared for being shouted at by her for not being at school. I can't remember what I said. Still, I'm sure it was unkind of me – I'm sorry mum, I love you.

Mum knows that I am proud of her for leaving him. She deserved better, but that's the challenge of controlling abusive relationships; the abuser usually holds all the cards and power. I struggled at first that she did not take me with her. Dad eventually became less stressed and more relaxed. We ended up having a pretty decent relationship for a couple of years until he re-married. The arguments disappeared. I was essentially left to my own devices. I'm not even sure my dad knew where my school was; I guess we both didn't care.

He'd started dating. I wonder how parents in the 80s met each other. Lonely hearts adverts? He had several girlfriends. I remember one, she stayed over a lot, 'whatever' her name; let's call her Janet. Janet, was a tall slim blonde woman with no kids and about 40 years of age, I guess. Janet arrived at the house early one evening before dad was home from work. After about an hour, she telephoned my dad at work. He came home quickly. This was the first time I'd ever seen him come early from work and because he'd been asked to! He came home, they went upstairs, there was crying and shouting, but not like it was with mum. A bit more subdued, like they didn't want me to hear. I heard swearing and my mum's name mentioned.

It turned out Janet had come home to find that someone had been through her clothes and her new shoes had been filled full of shaving foam. As far as I knew, it wasn't me, and the only other person who had been in the house was mum when she dropped me off after school. Had she done this? I took the blame and was shouted at, but they never believed me. I've always been a lousy liar, it was quite funny. I assumed then as I do now that it was mum, but the other choice is that Janet did it herself to blame either me or mum. If I was Janet, I probably wouldn't have wanted his ex-wife visiting the house either. I guess I'll know one way or another if mum ever reads this! If you did mum, you made me laugh. I never got hit for it when I took the blame.

Eventually, Dad and Janet split up, but within weeks, he had a new girlfriend, Marie. Marie was a divorcee from Wigan, again no kids, but for any faults she had, she was always kind to me from day one. Once Marie moved in, things stayed calm for a matter of weeks. I sat with her one day whilst she cried her heart out. I was about 13 or 14 and took the day off school. She was confused as dad had started to shout at her. Marie would spoil me rotten (with dad's credit card card!) and we went shopping after a bit to Wigan and eat lunch, I even had my hair cut in a salon – I came out red-faced and fat still, nothing like the photo of the model they showed me in the hairstyle book. We sat in a coffee shop whilst Marie cried again. "Why does he shout," she asked and, "Has he always been like this?"

I told her about him, warts and all, she was raging. Her way of coping is similar to mine now, she went out and drained the Visa card. A new three-piece sofa was ordered and a £100 Tracksuit for me! My mate's jaws hit the ground when I turned up to the Friday night breakdancing session in the road underpass. I loved Marie, and not because of the gifts. 'Good' things never last forever, and it's not like today with an app where things are 'hidden'. The bills started to arrive, and then the debt collectors would knock on the door, and then more arguments.

I was back to square one with the shouting and hitting. Except he had now discovered the face of his wife as a target to hit. He wore Marie down so much, one day she came down to breakfast with black eyes behind sunglasses and an excuse of migraine and sinus trouble (which she did have too) Marie stopped talking for about three weeks. She *was* trying to talk, all the movements was there, but no words came out. He'd broken her, the bastard.

"I'm home," I shouted as I came in the house from school, mud on my trainers and Marie was brushing it up behind me! The house was too quiet. "Spot! Here boy," Spot my dog would sit with me whilst I ate my tea and then would lie on my bed afterwards. Marie had become pregnant a month earlier. "Philip, sit down," Marie asked me nicely. She looked so nervous, you could cut the atmosphere with a knife. A bad guilty feeling hung in the air. Dad stood there, belly hanging over his belt.

"Spot has gone, it is for the best," he said matter of factly. "What do you mean gone? Where is he? When is he coming back? Has he been in accident?" "No the vet has put him to sleep today." "We can't have a dog in the house with a baby." "No!" I cried through tears. I squared up to my dad

137

and threw a punch. He moved; my fist went right through the wall and left a hole in the plasterboard. The light started to narrow in my vision. What do I do now? Marie was shaking

and crying at the kitchen table. I felt like a monster, but I wasn't the one who had just killed my dog. I turned and walked out of the kitchen past the first hole and stooped low under the stairs where Spot's bed was still placed in a plastic dog basket filled with blankets. I knelt down and curled up in the bed, a fat teen shaking and crying. I spent the rest of the week sleeping in Spot's bed basket under the stairs.

I wanted to die, but all I had for ideas were a diet of Hill Street Blues and Dirty Harry mixed in with the VHS craze. I had a limited list of sources for suicide choices. There was nothing in the Britannia encyclopaedia collection we owned. But I decided I wanted to die. What was the point? My best friend was gone. I made a mental list of four ways to die in Skem. This was more about the anger and me wanting to get over just how much they'd hurt me, but here's the list I made.

- Overdose – I was 12, I only had cough medicine. Cavonia wouldn't do it!
- Hanging – which 12-year-old has a rope!? I didn't.
- Cut my wrists and sit in the bath – I'd seen that in a film.
- Jump off a bridge – I'm scared of heights... and how high a bridge should it be?

Everyone was sleeping, I rolled out of Spot's bed and went to the kitchen. It was very dark, except for the street lamp outside of the kitchen window. I opened the cutlery draw, and took out a wooden handled Chinese meat cleaver. Dad kept it very sharp with a sharpening steel. I had decided to cut my wrists

I sat down at the kitchen table shaking and felt sick, but no tears came. I could 'see' Spot sat in front of me with that daft let's go for walk look on his face'. I then felt the cold metal of the kitchen knife on my wrist – do I just cut the skin? How far and, how do I get through the bone? Blood appeared, I put the Cleaver down onto the table, said sorry to Spot and told him I loved him but I couldn't do it. I fell asleep in the kitchen – what a coward.

When dad was dying from lung cancer, he asked me for forgiveness. I reminded him of killing my dog and made it clear I loved him, but equally, I hated what he'd done to me, and that he didn't have my forgiveness. He died later that night at his home with my sisters by his side. I'd never seen anyone die before. I next saw him lying in the undertakers in his clothes. "It didn't have to be like this," I told him quietly. I held his hand, it wasn't cold or warm. Oddly, I had expected it to be ice cold.

"All you had to do was be nice, and love us, but you let something in your past stop you and I'm not becoming you and I hate you for it and for how you treated Claire. She was your last chance. People don't often get another chance, but you messed that up too. She will do fine, but not because of you, but because of herself." I wept a little for myself as we did have some good times, and I wanted more. "Goodbye Dad, say Hi to Spot from me, and I'll see you again one day."

Around the time Spot was killed, mum had moved in with Eddie, her new boyfriend. He was two people in one and turned out to be quite mentally ill. I don't say this lightly or with any clinical knowledge. It's just bloody obvious looking back that he wasn't stable.

Eddie got violent with me near the end of their relationship, but we got on most of the time. Eddie was a motorcycle and car engine engineer, and like me, a fan of boxing and anything mechanical like bicycles. He had vinyl records of motorcycle engine noises and would one minute listen to Maria Callas and the next the aria of a BSA Gold Star at full revs! He had spells of mania, I believe, and could go from incredible highs to lows, but the in-between would be incredibly creative. I can recall him showing me a letter of acknowledgement from Rolls Royce for an engine he designed along with demonstrating a working model of how the crankshaft and piston were unique. I can't remember the detail and never really understood it then, but I am still hugely impressed. He had the type of mind that could probably understand Quantum Mechanics without a PHD or Math degree from reading one book.

Dad was born in Malaya in 1935, the son of a plantation owner. He was the middle child of four, two sisters and a younger brother. They have all passed on now. Dad, I believe, came over to England in August 1958. I am unclear if he came over as part of work or not; he had served in the British Army until the move, holding the rank of 2nd Lieutenant in the Far East Forces (Dec '56 – Aug '58). He'd also had a stint in Malaya working in the Merchant Navy (White Star Line) and also with Shell Oil. Mum is British and was born in 1944 in Chester). I was about 12 when I became aware that I was the last in the family to find out dad had been married before. I had another brother and sister living in London. It is not my story to tell why he left them and their mum when they were young. They have told me, but I will not comment here.

I was born in Hoylake in 1970, Wirral, now and a leafy middle-class area famous for being the Royal Liverpool Golf Club's home. I was born at home in what was affectionately known as the Pigeon's Nest. I'm told the Pigeon's Nest was the converted attic of a tall Victorian house that had been turned into a bedroom. The ground floor was a shop that they perhaps owned or operated.

We moved at some point, I think into a bungalow in Great Sutton (still the Wirral) and then to Garston in South Liverpool, possibly via Chester. We had a collie dog at this time too: Petra

Garston was a big old terrace end house. I must have been about five at most, as I had just started infant school. The ground floor of the house had a shop (stationery, I think) which mum and dad ran. Opposite was a small community hospital where mum also worked, I'm not sure as what, maybe as a healthcare assistant as she also did stints with St John's Ambulance service. Downstairs was a back room and big fireplace, and the kitchen was an extension out to the yard, which housed the coal shed and outdoor toilet.

I have a few mixed memories of that yard: two vivid ones are of me sitting on my knees with everyone around me whilst I held Petra, our dog, across my lap as she lay dying after being knocked over by a car. Petra was a beautiful black collie, and that was another sad moment of my life involving a dog. The next memory is a bit unclear. It is of my two cousins from Scotland (Colin and David) on my dad's side. Their mum (Molly) was dad's sister, and they had come to visit. Colin and David were both older than me. I'd have said they were a lot of older, but I've recently met up with them both again, and they aren't much older. My elder sister Vicky and big brother Chris were all messing around, and I don't know if it was exactly like this. Still, I remember it being a large 'olly' (marble) that Chris threw at the two cousins – maybe it wasn't a marble as it sounds like a crap game if it was – and doomed to end in disaster with one of us getting 'belted'. Anyway, it went smashing through the window behind them into the back room of the house.

I knew as soon as the window smashed, one of us would get Dad's belt across our backside, not the greatest of deterrents! I am not one of those people that looks on such times fondly and says, "That is what they did then, and it did me no harm." It was cruel and barbaric, and I fucking hated him for it. I got the belt then – as well as for at least the next ten years every time he was angry. I was always a 'latch key kid', from a young age. I can recall going into an empty derelict house around the corner from our home in Garston near the fish and chip shop when I was about 5. Of course, I had been warned not to, but where is the fun in that? Kids need to get up to no good and have some danger and risk in their lives. I do get mad but secretly admire my kids when they ignore me and get up to mischief – but please don't tell them!

I admire the Japanese 'First Errand' tradition, where they send their child out into the world from a very young age (as young as three sometimes) to perform an errand like shopping for themselves and develop independence!'

Well now, back to my story. It was a creepy old derelict house; I suspect now gentrified and over-priced, but back in 1975, I found a drunk old man wrapped in cardboard. "Fuck off!!" he' bellowed, at the same time drinking from a bottle; 'old or drunk Billy,' I think he was called. I remember just wanting to talk to him before becoming frightened and running home as fast as I could. Billy was always hanging around the area drunk and scruffy. Kids being kids had made up terrible stories about him and called him names, other silly memories from about 1974/5: chips were circa 25p a portion (bag). Why were they called a bag of chips? They never came in a bag, and a Mars bar was about 2.5p!

One summers evening, I wandered up the side road of our house to the large grass park area. Chris was there with some friends. They were hitting golf balls with a seven iron club. I stood and watched, but either I got too close, or he did it on purpose – I like to think it was the former – but on one swing, he smashed the club across my head as he swung down, slitting open my ear. I can't remember which ear it was. Still, I remember mum taking me to the hospital, I assume the one that stood over the road from our house. I can still feel the stinging when I recall it, boy o boy.

We moved to Skelmersdale from Garston in the mid to late 70s.

Chapter 10: Leaving School

I hated high school. My recollection of it is as a period of being called names and being unhappy.

"Hi," I said as I waved to the man in the Ford Cortina. It was an involuntary wave. I was just being too polite to someone I thought I knew. Had I realised it was the deputy headmaster, I would have turned the other way.

Instead of attending my O level examinations, I had decided to go fishing instead! I was sat at the side of the road on top of my wicker fishing basket, waiting for my mate and his dad to give us a lift. I felt sick as I realised what I had done. 'I've gotten away with it', I thought, as the headmaster did not stop.

"Where have you been all day?" Demanded my dad. "Fishing at the canal, then I went into school to finish my exams, why?" I realised what was happening, but was in my teenage 'I know best' angst-ridden mood. "The school and the council have been on the phone. They say you have only been in school for half of this year. They are threatening to get the police involved, you must start attending."

"I have been to school," I pleaded as though this was all a huge surprise and an affront to me! You have seen the letters about the teacher strikes and why I haven't been able to attend," I argued confidently. Nobody had questioned the validity of my homemade photocopied letters to date, they really were very good. I had copied and pasted the school's letterhead onto blank paper and, in my dad's office at his warehouse, typed a letter. I had then photocopied it so that it looked more authentic with that school-like black toner shadow down one side of the paper.

I used to spend my time either roaming the streets, fishing or with Neil bunking off school right at the bottom of his garden! We would creep into an old caravan Neil's family had and spend the day whilst his dad would be at work.

"The school say they haven't sent any letters home for months and that you've copied old letters and lied to us all!" I was caught. There was nothing else to do but to cry and try to get some sympathy. I did so and explained how unhappy I was, being fat and called names. Dad was sympathetic, but offered no advice. It was a case of 'suck it up' and get back to school. As far as I know, he never spoke to the school about my feelings. I can see now my modus operandi was set early in life to run away from problems that I did not want to face.

After leaving school, I decided to go to college. I was now living with mum and her boyfriend, Eddie. I eventually decided to do a City and Guilds catering course. I was overjoyed when Neil decided to also join the same course at the same college in Southport. This was going to be fun, I thought. I was excited. We both bought small learner motorcycles so that we could get to college easily. I really admire my mum for supporting me to buy a motorbike. It must have been difficult for her to see me ride off wobbly for the first time! I hope I can do the same for my kids one day!

Unlike high school, college was interesting. I chose catering to become a chef. My best mate Neil came on the course too, and what a blast we had. I hated the management side of the training and learning about running a dining room. I just wanted to cook! Life was hard at that time for me. Mum lived with a new partner, and I'd moved in. I enjoyed great freedom. My heavy interest lay in two things: Martial Arts and motorbikes. Eddie being a motor racing engineer meant I had the only tuned 125cc motorbike around! I had also turned my bedroom into a mini dojo with kick bags and weapons, and Eddie had crafted a makiwara in the garden for me.

The makiwara (巻藁) is a padded striking post used as a training tool in various styles of traditional karate. It is thought to be uniquely Okinawan in origin. The makiwara is one form of Hojo undō, a method of supplementary conditioning used by Okinawan martial artists.

The thing about Eddie was, he had incredible mood swings. I had a dog at the time, Rocky, a Weimaraner. One Sunday I was hungover and asleep, but Rocky had been out into the side yard of the house and done a poop, as dogs do.

I'd normally come down to clean the poop up once I had woken up and pop it in the chemical bin we had.

This morning was different. I was confused and disoriented being woken up to a carving knife pointed to my face by Eddie. he was clearly having a bad morning! He then reached towards me with a stick with the dog poo on it and wiped it on me and my bedclothes. His eyes were wide and crazed with wispy hair on his head swept back. I think the knife was stopping me from reacting. Eddie had worked with his hands his whole life and was incredibly strong. I wasn't about to try his strength out. I got a shower then went downstairs. I confronted him then, but he still had a crazed look in his eyes.

"Fuck you I'm going to kill you," I screamed as I grabbed a knife in the kitchen and went for him. He grabbed me, I hit a sideboard with my back as he pushed me backwards. He was holding my wrist tightly. My forearm was straining and sore. I dropped the knife, and we wrestled until I was out of energy.

Later that week, mum and I packed our bags. Mum went to live near one of my sisters Vicky in the Midlands. I had to leave the house. I bummed around first staying with my brother in Sandhurst at the military officers training school, but after a few months, I ended up back with my dad and his new wife and a very young child. I dropped out of college and went to work.

Chapter 11: Work

I had many jobs in my 20s, all mainly involving transport and sales. I've delivered coffins across the country, undertaken back-breaking house moves and helped people set up small businesses all from my kitchen table!

Through a friend, I got an interview as a forklift driver at a pizza factory. After all, how hard could driving a forklift be? I turned up nervous. The Transport Manager was Margaret, which was highly unusual for the time in a male-dominated industry where every warehouse toilet had a well-stocked supply of pornographic magazines, as did the walls in the restrooms. I turned up in a shirt and tie and my best Lee jeans. There was no YouTube to do a crash course on forklift driving, but Margaret was a mate's wife. Alan told me, "It was a shoe-in," meaning, just turn up, don't crash, and the job is yours.

A friend at another firm had a gas-powered forklift truck and let me practice at the weekends in the yard. Forward and back and spin around and then up and down, not that hard. In fact, I was a natural.

But on the day of the interview, I failed miserably and ended up lying through my teeth about how different the truck was to the ones I'd driven before. This machine though was electric and not only went up and down and around, but you could move the forks in and out. The truck moved sideways too. Being electric, it needed very light touches.

The test was I had to put on a cold suit, suitable for freezing temperatures. I was shaking as I put on the hard hat and gloves. I was to drive into a cold storage freezer with a list of pallets to collect for the truck, I was then to load them in reverse delivery order into the refrigerated 40 ft lorry, which was waiting on the loading bay. I managed one pallet successfully, a fluke! But mates are mates, and I was given the job and a wake-up call to life!

I was the 'food freezer store man', which meant I looked after the stock in and out of the freezer, including the pre-prepared pizza ingredients which were kept on sample boxes on a rack in the freezer, bit like pizza topping 'pick 'n mix'. The lads in the factory were all on the 'make' and all sold knock off gear (stolen items) to each other. In the first two days, I was offered trainers, suits and coke (not the cola) when the R&D person in the office (a German food technician named Bodo) requested items from the 'pick 'n mix' for a new recipe. He would send down a list of what he needed as well as the type of frozen pizza base to send up. The lads came to me with the order.

The safety protocols meant that I had to escort them into the freezer. A fully insulated arctic type snowsuit is worn in the freezer, so when he dropped his pants after I unlocked the freezer, it didn't surprise me. You normally put it on over your clothes, but I was new, so what the hell, I thought. When he dropped his trousers outside the huge metal door, I was nervous and a bit scared of them all. If the truth be told, we all came from the same area, but I sounded like an educated snob compared to them. I could string a sentence together without the word fuck, and I didn't have kids with three different women.

He suited up and I put the pizza base requested next to the ingredient rack. The lad – I'll call him Paul (I don't remember his exact name) – unzipped his suit and dropped it around his ankles. I watched in confused bewilderment. Was this some sort of initiation test, I wondered? No that was still to come! He then took the pizza base and rubbed the base across his testicles then anus. He got dressed again, started to gather all of the ingredients into the sample pot, but before taking it upstairs, he left a healthy dose of phlegm and snot in it.

I spoke with him later and explained how stupid it was. I was pushed into an office window by three of the lads in the warehouse. They explained if I opened my mouth, I'd be flying through the window next time. There is something really intimidating and believable about a strong local accent, so I believed them. They couldn't give a shit about the job or pay, but they did give a shit about their side-line of selling stolen stuff to each other and drugs to drivers.

The next day, I arrived at the factory at 8am as normal, nervous and frightened. I checked the manifest for the day. It had been altered. I was on cleaning duty for the afternoon. I had been trained in this as part of my induction by Margaret and the warehouse manager. It involved a steel cage being attached to one of the warehouse forklifts. Later that afternoon, I stepped into the cage with my safety boots on, hardhat and climbing harness. I was then attached with a safety strap to the cage and given cleaning materials. The warehouse manager then lifted the cage up with the unit shaking to the ceiling where I would take off the covers of the large lights and proceed to wipe them down before fitting them back.

This went on for about two hours. I called down as I needed a break and a drink, but there was no response; it was about 3pm. It turns out this was the initiation test. I quickly realized what was going on and shouted for help. I had been left in the cage at the top of the warehouse whilst all of the warehouse lads had gone out. I never knew where they went. Bodo and Margaret eventually came out of the offices down the steel staircase and across the warehouse floor, gently lowering me in the cage. They were full of apologies but explained it was just the lads' way of bonding with me! I knew they had no idea what they were all like. I got changed, had a shower, and got in my car to finish early for the day. I never went back to that place again. I actually drove to North

Wales and had an afternoon out in my car and visiting friends of my dad's whom I had known ever since I could remember.

Saturday morning, we would all sit in the warehouse of my new employer, Amtrak parcels. I was before the regional sales rep and a national sales manager who had come to speak to us all about the business. It was a franchise business, and the owner was very secretive. I'm not sure how I was ever given the job as we never really got on, including during the interview, but it paid well enough that I could afford with my fiancé Kate to rent a converted farmhouse in the countryside. It was our first place together.

Saturday morning meeting, it went well. The sales manager explained that the company owner always welcomed new ideas and that we should let him know if we had any. I had been working on an idea as to how to deliver clothing for retail in a way that meant it never got creased. This was a long time before Amazon had been conceived. I wrote to the owner of the company in Bristol with my idea and operating procedures. About three weeks later, my manager met with me along with the national sales manager, and the owner of Amtrak was on a call with me. The owner explained he really liked the idea but felt it was ahead of its time and would require too much investment.

After the call and after the sales manager departed the office, my manager went ballistic, throwing a cup against the wall and smashing it! I laughed as it looked quite pathetic.

154

"Never do anything like that again," he said. It turned out he was in legal disputes with the owner of Amtrak regarding the contract terms, and it didn't want to do anything that would help the company. We had words and I told him where to stick his job and went home.

Over the next few years, I worked successfully for what was then one of the leading parcel courier companies, Interlink and the then business post and the failed, Next Day. I have always enjoyed being in a sales role. You are very much the master of your own destiny and can see the benefits of your efforts in the form of enhanced pay through commission.

At Interlink, we were given our vehicles to take home. I always felt this was to compensate for the poor salaries we were all paid. We were not insured to use the vehicles in our own time, but of course, everybody did. We just put a bit of petrol in to keep the boss happy. A few of my co-workers also used their van to operate private transport companies in the evenings and weekends, something I had no interest in doing.

It was a Friday night. We had been to Wigan to a girl's house listening to records and flirting with her and her friends. Two small learner motorcycles were revving behind me in the van. My two soul mates Neil and Steve were in the passenger seat. I 'hit' the apex perfectly and drifted out towards the right to attack the next bend. Thud! I hit the curb as I went for the next apex. My steering went light and instead of hitting the 'point', I had found the curb.

I assume the weight transfer and high center of gravity for a van changed the dynamics from my dad's car I was used to driving in the evenings. I wrestled with the steering but could see we were looking down at speed. The van pivoted in the air and spun but onto four wheels again, now facing 90-degrees to the right. It lurched across the road and through a wall on a bridge (no exaggeration). We went through a fucking stone wall on a bridge before sliding down an embankment in the van until the motion was stopped by trees and bushes yards from the river. This all happened in a second or two. I don't know how we all climbed out of the van. The lads on the motorbikes Fizzies (a Fizzy was a Suzuki 50cc 2 stroke motorcycle with the model name Fs1e, hence fizzy!) asked if we were okay. We all nodded that its okay – it was a 'now don't fucking say anything, nod' kind of a nod. They rode off in a haze of lovely 2 stroke perfume.

The three of us were 'okay'. There was a pub over the road, and someone must have called the police. It was 1988/9, no mobile phones for the masses yet! Police and ambulance arrived, checked us all out. There was a bit of glass in my hair. Neil and Steve got a ride in the ambulance to the hospital, and I got a ride in the police car – we did the statement stuff. I admitted driving like a nob, etc. Apparently, this was stupid of me to be honest, according to the insurers. And people say it is drivers defraud the insurance industry. None of us claimed for the accident, despite Neil's dad wanting him to sue me. It wouldn't have mattered to me, of course. His dad was right, but suing your mate is not very matey, is it? I knew he wouldn't, and he didn't!

I had bad dreams and flashbacks for years following that event. I was scared I'd killed my mates or ran over a pedestrian with her baby, destroying other lives. I went to see the van at a garage where the insurance assessed it, it was like a concertina (over 50% of the width had gone), and the whole engine had been pushed back into the cabin. Where I sat, the garage told me a tree had torn through the windscreen. They assumed I'd died in the crash and were amazed anyone walked away. I threw up outside the garage and cried a lot! It was the firm's van and my boss was great telling me over a cup of tea and a sarnie in a cafe that I'd fucked up and should be sacked, but that he was young once and that this event would save my life because I wouldn't do it again. He handed me the keys to a brand new van. In his broad scouse accent, he said, "Now Pat, don't fucking crash this one, you cunt!"

We laughed and we walked back to the depot. The boss's dad worked there too. He came over to me. "So has he sacked you? You daft prick?!" He was raging on Richard the boss, his son, for not sacking me at first, but then explained he'd raised him to be kind, so he was proud I got another chance.

In case you're wondering, I went by the name Pat as there were three other Phils at the company! And I was the youngest and newest! Apparently, it was never an issue till I joined!

About a month later, one of the drivers, a big thin bloke Paul, and then another Paul and a guy called Roy said, "Pat, can we have a chat round the back of the building?" It wasn't really a question. I went around to the back of the building with them. I knew what was coming and was ready. My body was tensing up. I wasn't sure why, but after years of being hit as a kid, I just instinctively knew this meeting wasn't to ask me if I was okay.

I put my keys in my fist, poking out between my fingers as an improvised weapon. I knew I was going to get a kicking, but some things you just have to take like a man, and this was one of them. I just didn't know why. Okay, sure, I'd been flirting with tall Paul's girlfriend, but everyone did! 20 blokes and one young female – everyone fancied her.

The shorter stocky Paul spun round when I stopped walking. He was right up in my face. He got my jacket by the scruff of the neck and hoisted me up off the ground! I was pushed back into the warehouse unit wall. In-between threats of breaking bits of me which was all very un-menacing, they tried to explain that my accident was the 'one' that pushed the insurers to raise Richard's premiums to a point where our monthly delivery bonus might now not be paid. I was given a talking too and a warning, a gentle 'dig' in the ribs and a slap. They did the right thing. I believe in a strong word and a slap. And you know what, I didn't crash again that year. I did years after, but I'll just leave it there.

This was another major life lesson for me. This time, about the impact of your actions on others. They were all grown men with families, and while this job might have paid crappy money, it was all they had, and they were going to fight for it. I started to change my attitude and ended up getting on really well with the lads and accompanied a lot of laughs along the way.

Chapter 12: Maternity Scandal – "A Lethal Mix of Failures"

"It's a Shit List, boss."

"A what?"

"It's all the things I think could now happen to the Trust, and put simply, it's a Shit List!" I bet you won't find this on any fancy crisis communications training course!

The list included everything from the CEO being sacked and the whole board removed through to a public enquiry. I'd never managed something like this before, but I knew we needed to be prepared for what might come and require a communications response. I must apologise as babies and a mother unnecessarily died and my language was not acceptable given the gravity of the matter.

It was 2012, and I was asked to become the Head of Communications for the Trust. I had no training in crisis communications, but I welcomed the role as I felt my values and beliefs would serve me well. The Morecambe Bay Investigation: commonly known as 'The Kirkup Report', had yet to be conceived. But as you can see, it wasn't a surprise to me when it was announced. I had already planned for it and expected it from a communications perspective. In fact, that isn't the complete truth. I had expected a public enquiry, with the full legal powers that are bestowed upon an enquiry. But despite the Kirkup investigation not being a public enquiry, it was certainly thorough, and turned over all the stones that needed turning.

I was sat at home at the kitchen table, a 1-year-old baby on my knee, both having fun on a Saturday morning. The inquest into the unnecessary death of baby Joshua Titcombe after being born at Furness General Hospital had been held two weeks ago, and since there had been a flurry of media attention and further regulatory inspections with a damning report ensuing from the care quality commission and also the nursing and midwifery council (NMC), the attention was to be expected and was certainly warranted. I was caught out on the national interest in it, as were the rest of the NHS.

The inquest for Joshua, as reported by the Guardian newspaper claimed:

"Joshua Titcombe died at nine days old from a common infection that could have been cured by antibiotics after medical staff repeatedly ignored his parents' fears for his health and told them "not to worry."[2]

A phone call on this morning had come from a member of the communications team. "Phil, SKY News are outside Furness General Hospital, and they want an interview on the report and the inquest."

---

2 The Guardian. (2011). Joshua Titcombe Inquest Cumbria Coroner. Retrieved from
https://www.theguardCraig.com/society/2011/jun/07/joshua-titcombe-inquest-cumbria-coroner

"Okay it's a reasonable request, but we have already given interviews and it isn't something that couldn't wait till Monday morning," I pushed back for discussion. "I don't think they're going away, Phil they are set up with cameras and a satellite van on the main road. The staff will be getting very anxious and we have pregnant mums having to walk past it and into the maternity unit."

"That is a very good point, thank you. We do have to consider the public's feelings and I don't want mothers getting any more anxious as that will be unhealthy for them and their babies. Are they interviewing anybody else?"

"They haven't said, but I will ask again," said my colleague,

"Give me 15 minutes please to arrange some things, and I'll get back to you if you stay at the office at Furness General Hospital." I called the regional NHS Strategic Health Authority Communications lead for some advice "Phil, if they don't have anyone else to talk, don't give them an interview, they are a television station and will soon go away if they don't have any 'talking heads'," I was told.

I didn't feel comfortable with this. My instinct was to be transparent, provide an interview and then ask them to leave. I saw it as another opportunity to reach out and reassure the public and expectant mothers. I spoke to the CEO and relayed everything to him. I told him my opinion. He was out walking his dog at the time. He said he wanted to go with the advice of the local Strategic Health Authority and turned down the interview request. I thought about this and instead telephoned the Medical Director. He was in church delivering a reading, but even so, he saw my number and came out. I explained the position and the CEO decision, but I didn't believe this was the end of it. This matter was much too serious, and as a national TV station had made the effort of turning up on a Saturday morning, I didn't believe they would just turn around and drive off.

Turned out, I was right, as they stayed for another two weeks. So I asked the medical Director to jump in a car and meet me at the hospital. I would prepare a statement for him. He did that, he changed his family and church plans. He was always willing to drop everything and step up.

About two hours later, we met at the hospital. My phone and that of the CEO was red-hot. Most of the NHS hierarchy had now been made aware of the new significant media interest, and they were all encouraging an interview to be given to calm the situation down as live reports would be broadcast from the 'scandal-hit maternity hospital'. However, none them offered to provide an interview themselves! Their change in recommendation was at odds with their previous communications advice. My colleague had prepared the statement lines for me whilst I had driven to the hospital. We had them cleared by the regional NHS communications director and prepared for our Medical

Director to deliver a short statement live on the news, this was to be delivered together with a phone number for any anxious people to call where a midwife would talk to them about any worries they might have.

The statement focused on clarifying what happened and then what has and is being done about the findings. I wanted the Trust to take a 'mea culpa' position and come out admitting wrongdoing. The rest of the senior team were uncomfortable with this, as everybody was still very defensive about the coroner's findings who had reported that on balance, Joshua's medical records had not merely gone missing but likely had been destroyed deliberately by the midwives involved in his care. I felt we shouldn't be challenging the coroner as we have no evidence to do so and the fact that the coroner had come to this decision after a thorough examination of all the facts. The statement was delivered, and as expected, it was a tough interview. I thought the interview was fair, but when you are only used to being interviewed by local newspapers, this was a different level altogether. The usual trite lines of 'learning lessons' wasn't going to cut it with a more experienced journalist who deals with crisis situations on a more regular basis.

My communications manager and I set up the office for what turned out to be the best part of the next six months in the major incident room at Furness General Hospital. We treated it as a major incident, invoking the procedures helped us receive further support in the shape of an administrator to log and record all our actions and decisions from here on in. We were also able to recruit additional members of the team to assist as the hours were much too long to sustain without illness or holiday. It was clear to me that at some point, everything would be forensically examined, and people will be held accountable. It wasn't from a defensive position I decided this, it was from a professional and transparent position so that at a later date, our actions could be scrutinised. I'm very conscious that we are paid by the public through taxation.

What did I learn? You can't under-resource a communications crisis. The crisis was bigger than communications, but I was dealing in communications, that was my responsibility, and we were woefully understaffed and under-invested in. It's a function that can often be seen in some NHS, as a cost rather than an investment. Some other Trusts were like our Trust back then, unwisely treating it as the Department that just sends out press releases and pretty newsletters and answers the odd journalist enquiry from the local newspaper. More professional and mature organisations realise it is a strategic function to communicate and assist with communicating and engaging the workforce and stakeholders on the direction of the organisation as well as the timely communication from the Trust Board on key matters. Then there is the need to plan for crisis communication situations.

 Great change didn't come about until the then Secretary of State for Health, Jeremy Hunt, announced an independent investigation into the maternity failings at the Trust. The report was published in 2015 and was led by Dr Bill Kirkup CBE

Dr Bill Kirkup describes the issues best:

"For the great majority, pregnancy and childbirth should be a positive and happy experience that culminates in a healthy mother and baby. This means, however, that on those occasions when things do go wrong, the effects are even more devastating than in other areas of healthcare. Maternity care must reconcile these dual aspects in order to be safe, effective and responsive. When it does not, the consequences may be stark. This Report details a distressing chain of events that began with serious failures of clinical care in the maternity unit at Furness General Hospital, part of what became the University Hospitals of Morecambe Bay NHS Foundation Trust. The result was avoidable harm to mothers and babies, including tragic and unnecessary deaths. What followed was a pattern of failure to recognise

the nature and severity of the problem, with, in some cases, denial that any problem existed, and a series of missed opportunities to intervene that involved almost every level of the NHS. Had any of those opportunities been taken, the sequence of failures of care and unnecessary deaths could have been broken. As it is, they were still occurring after 2012, eight years after the initial warning event, and over four years after the dysfunctional nature of the unit should have become obvious."

My role at the hospital Trust via reporting to the CEO was to lead the Trust's Communications response to the Kirkup Investigation. Before that, first as the Trust's Marketing Manager, then when I returned from Adoption leave, I took over as the Head of Corporate Communications.

I tell myself that the previous CEO and the Board weren't bad people in the period 2010-12 when most of the failures started to be reported on. But you know what, when you sign that piece of paper and take the money, being paid many times more than the rank and file in the organisation, then the buck stops there. So no, they were not all bad people, but they didn't do the right thing either, and collectively they are accountable. What I observed was a male-dominated Executive Team with a clear dominant male pack leader. An Akela, if you like. He was not challenged, a talented bunch, individually perhaps, but collectively they lacked the 'bite'. Therefore they are responsible and accountable for the terrible and sometimes fatal mistakes that were made, in my opinion.

In 2010, the hospital Trust was chasing the goal of becoming an 'NHS Foundation Trust' It is important to remember what an NHS Foundation Trust is/meant to be:

Foundation trusts are a different type of NHS organisation with a stronger local influence.

Foundation trust hospitals are still part of the NHS and treat patients according to NHS principles of free healthcare according to need, not the ability to pay. Being a foundation trust means that Trust's should be better able to provide and manage its services to meet the needs and priorities of the local community, as the Trust is free from central Government control.

Foundation trusts are different from standard NHS trusts in three important ways. They:

- *have freedom to decide locally how to meet their obligations.*
- *are accountable to local people, who can become members and governors.*
- *are authorised and monitored by an independent regulator for NHS foundation trusts*

However, foundation trusts are still be accountable to Parliament. The freedoms given to NHS foundation trusts are underpinned by a framework of national standards which safeguard quality and protect the public interest.

In essence, they were granted the autonomy to operate in a more 'business'-like way, free of some of the bureaucracy that existed to make their own decisions and for the public to have a greater say through pseudo-'shareholders' in the shape of a voluntary Board of Governors who don't have any day-to-day operational power or responsibility, and the public to become 'members'. The Governors hold the Chair and non-executive to account, and the non-executives Directors hold the executive Directors to account, or that's the theory at least.

Let me cite the Kirkup Report again:

14. A member of NW SHA [Regional NS Strategic Health Authority] staff questioned whether there was a gap in understanding of the five 2008 incidents, and whether they should be investigated. These were the right questions, but in implementing what became the Fielding review, the Trust not only shifted the emphasis away from what had happened and onto current systems, but also instructed Dame Pauline Fielding not to investigate the incidents. Despite stating that the review had not re-examined the incidents, the Fielding Report unwisely stated that they appeared "coincidental rather than evidence of serious dysfunction." This was easily misread as a finding of the review and was widely misunderstood as a result.

15. The review report was produced in draft in March 2010, but what was described as minor redrafting took until August 2010 to finalise. It contained significant criticisms of the Trust's maternity care, including dysfunctional relationships, poor environment and a poor approach to clinical governance and effectiveness. The report was given very limited circulation within the Trust and was not shared with the NW SHA until October 2010, or with the CQC and Monitor until April 2011. Although we heard different accounts, and it was clear that there was limited managerial capacity to deal with a demanding agenda, including the FT application, we found on the balance of probability that there was an element of conscious suppression of the report both internally and externally. This was a further significant missed opportunity.

I have some late experience of the Fielding report and its sharing, but details aside, I don't disagree with Dr Kirkup's findings. I am not qualified to comment on clinical practice, so I won't.

There are many more reports into what happened with failures at Morecambe Bay, but I believe Dr Kirkup's report to be presenting the definitive findings.

I believe the hospital chased the FT status as a 'prize' and sought, above everything else, as a sign of success and superiority and the regulator of the time Monitor, encouraged it. Everyone became 'blind' to what was failing under their noses with ego and pride taking over. Failings in maternity were known by the Trust before being awarded FT status. Dr Kirkup has shown this, but the NHS is a strange beast and people are still not, in my opinion, rewarded or incentivised for recognising problems; instead, they are often castigated.

The above extract is an appalling finding, the Trust believed their own hype, and to me, deliberately read the report how they felt it would best suit them. Five 'coincidences', let's think about that. It's not the number five, it makes me mad to see lives described as figures. It's five dead babies. I am conflicted in my criticism as I have a lot of respect for the then-Medical Director. He never hid when the going got tough. It comes back to accountability and responsibility. When SKY TV was 'banging on the door' requesting a live interview with Kay Burley on the prime-time news slot, it was the Medical Director who came forward and gave the interview. The CEO gave an excuse about how people wanted to hear from a doctor. The theory is fine, but in reality, I don't think people really care. They just want to know that the person at the top is taking responsibility for putting things right and owning up when they have gone wrong.

The CEO should have had the courage to stick his hand up and halt the FT process and say, "We need help, there is a problem, five Babies have died, and we need to understand why before we go any further. We must have everything focussed on making it safe and putting right the findings in the report." How can you ignore it? If he did say this and there is evidence for it, then I am sorry. But I've never yet seen it, and it appears neither did Dr Kirkup and his team of experts. Five babies died, and the connection is clear in my mind. It is that five babies have died in the same unit, end of argument. Death had become normalised. But the heart-breaking fact that should have kept them awake at night is the fact that five families will never spend another day with their children; that is the link, right there. It should have led to an independent forensic examination of practices and culture.

"How many of you have read the Fielding report, and know how my baby boy died, bleeding to death nine days later in a Newcastle hospital?" or words along these lines. The Trust Board all looked down at their hands as they sat around the table in the meeting room. It was James Titcombe, the father of Joshua, who had called out the question from the auditorium seats. I was sat just behind him, observing the board meeting as I was not a board member at this time. His challenge was entirely appropriate and warranted, I've heard people criticise James over the years, they were all wrong, I think he was very measured, me I'd have brought my baseball bat in and broken the table in two where they were sat! But the response he received was nothing short of disgusting. I wasn't embarrassed, I was sick. The chairman banged the table with a gavel, spouting that this was a meeting held in public, not a public meeting. Semantics as far as I'm concerned, we are holding a meeting in public and paid for by the public. I can't tell you as fact whether all of the board members had read the Fielding report or not, but it was clear, certainly from the non-executive directors who wouldn't look up, that they were confused and perplexed.

I made my own conclusion without any evidence other than the clear inability of any of them to answer a perfectly reasonable question from a bereaved father. If they can provide me with evidence of the contrary, I will stand corrected and apologise, but I wouldn't hold my breath waiting for it. I was later 'spoken to' by the Chair and CEO as to why I didn't know about the possible attendance of James. "It's a meeting open to the Public!" I explained, surprised that anyone was even annoyed with me. "They don't need to let us know in advance, and they sat at the front, they were not hiding." The CEO did state at the meeting that everybody had seen the report, but as you can see from the findings from Dr Kirkup, he drew the same conclusion as I did, and he stated so in his report:

Although we heard different accounts, and it was clear that there was limited managerial capacity to deal with a demanding agenda, including the FT application, we found on the balance of probability that there was an element of conscious suppression of the report both internally and externally. [Dr Kirkup, Fielding report comments]

Did the Directors deliberately hide the report? I do not know for certain, but they didn't go out of their way to share it either. Prior to a massive decision about the Trust's future, so on balance, I believe they did commit wilful blindness and suppressed sharing the report in a timely and proactive manner, and in doing so potentially caused further harm through an insufficient review. I believe all reports that are commissioned into the performance or safety of an NHS body or any other public body should be made public without the need for Freedom of Information requests. There may be some details, particularly around patients that might need to be removed, but I believe the public would accept and understand this if it were reasonably done. Although part of me struggles with that still, it's just more hiding of information.

My other lesson is that information will always find a way of coming out, be it now or in the days, weeks, months and years ahead. One thing is for certain, it will always come out. So don't wait for it to, publish it, get on the front foot and be honest. There will be occasions in a busy complex organisation where such things are missed. Be honest about it, don't try to spin it, and come up with reasons to justify it. Just tell the truth if you made a mistake and don't forget the word sorry. In the case of the Fielding report, excuses were made about the report being embedded in other reports to the regulator. I don't buy it. I heard lots of excuses, but I was never shown any evidence such as an email to the Regulator or commissioners saying 'here is a report'.

I find honesty and openness a strange concept in the NHS, as I believe it is often overly concerned with the politics and national reputation.

I have twice attended (in part) the national NHS Leadership Programme by Nye Bevan. These are meant to be the executive NHS leaders of tomorrow. I enjoyed the programme and made some good friends, but not once was I taught or lectured on the importance of openness and transparency, nor was there any understanding shown as to what reputation is. It comes from doing what you promise, pure and simple. The NHS and other bodies can spend a lot of time concentrating on the big things.

Still, as you have seen, it was the small things that made the biggest difference to my care and experience. It doesn't matter which NHS body it is, be it a local hospital or my GP surgery, if you send me an appointment saying you'll see me at 10am, I will be taking the morning off work, first to travel then to park and to arrive just before 10am so that I can be seen promptly. The promise that has been made to me in which the organization's reputation now hangs on is not the quality of the clinical care, but it is seeing me promptly at

10am, the rest, in my opinion, is an unwritten given, who doesn't expect to be treated safely and with care by a doctor or nurse? This is the very least we expect, so when that goes wrong, our unwritten contract has been broken. It is this that people will repeat to others and post on social media. Of course, the big things are important too.

People forget the first line of the NHS Constitution. It is powerful and clearly states that **"the NHS belongs to the people" [NHS England]**. It doesn't say it belongs to the managers or the government. It belongs to everybody, and I try to keep that basic tenet as my mantra and focal point in everything I do at work. I get it wrong a lot, and that hurts me. I know I can do better though.

I don't know where it comes from, this view of "don't tell." I honestly have never heard any of the executives at the time of the Maternity Scandal say, "Don't tell people this or that," but at the same time, press statements were poured over by the CEO and some Directors to 'spin' and deflect the truth. I did experience this through freedom of information requests, which were held back for longer than necessary whilst the CEO would ponder the need for additional information rather than letting the facts speak for themselves. And on one occasion, the CEO considering an injunction on a grieving widow and father to silence them.

I attended the inquest – wrongly, I believe, but – to understand the argument from a CEO as to why they may wish their comms leader to attend. I tried to put myself in the shoes of James Titcombe and his wife Hoa, and I wondered what sort of message does this send – that the Director of Nursing and the Medical Director or CEO were not in attendance, but two members of the communications team were, what does the Trust think is more important? Learning what it could do better or concentrating on its PR? I am not perfect, I make mistakes, and like the executives, I never 'won' an argument with the CEO either.

I was walking from the train station to the office one lovely sunny morning (but cold) walk into the hospital at Kendal where the directors are based. It is mostly a downhill walk for about 2 miles, first past some farm fields and into a nice new housing estate with a path that led into the back at the hospital via a small wooden bridge over a bubbling stream at the rear of the houses. My mobile phone rang as I entered the housing development. It was 8am and it was Tony the CEO. He was angry about press headlines, stating the Trust had the worst mortality figures for any NHS hospital in the country.

I tried to explain to him that the headlines were in fact correct whether he liked them or not, but he said he was now under pressure from the local NHS leaders about the headlines that were appearing, especially as it was coinciding with the reporting of the maternity failings and regulator report. It was at this time that Cumbria

Constabulary, who also attended the inquest, announced that they were launching a criminal investigation into the Trust, based on the regulator's report and what they had heard at the inquest. It was just the day before, and we had been rocked as a new unpublished report had been shared with the press ahead of an official publication a week early. I can't use the word leaked as I don't believe it is something that can be leaked. It is about the death of people and the public have a right to know. It turned out the Medical Director had written to all of his consultants explaining the poor results, which is the right thing to do in my opinion. What I would say, and it goes back to my comments about the Fielding report and it not being shared, is that as the head of communications I knew nothing about the mortality report being received by the Trust, nor had I been consulted on the letter that was sent to consultants.

The Trust really was poor at governance. It was possibly a naive decision to share an unpublished report with the medical body as hospital doctors were rightly very unhappy with how the Trust was being betrayed and performing in many areas. The letter they received was therefore shared with the press by a staff member, so not a leak as far as I'm concerned – just somebody doing the 'right thing'. It's not as though we didn't know what was in the report! And when I say we, you now know I don't mean me, as the first I heard was a journalist calling me the night before to tell me.

Mortality figures are a complex and emotive subject which are shrouded in mystery, and I find still that those responsible for the figures to be very defensive and aloof with a view someone like me might not be able to understand them! The data of it was making the headlines related to what is called HSMR data and was published regularly and via an annual report by a private medical data company called Dr Foster.

The reputed Imperial Hospitals describe HSMR well:

"The HSMR score is worked out by looking at performance in the NHS and adjusting the mortality risk in a spell of patient care for risk factors such as their age, gender and health conditions. The HSMR uses risk models to provide the number of 'expected deaths' per trust per month, compared with the number of actual deaths at the trust. This helps to produce the level of risk, called the 'relative risk figure' for each trust, which shows how each trust performs against the NHS average." [Imperial Hospitals]

Most people would expect that a specialist hospital such as a cancer hospital might experience more deaths in a given period than, say, a general hospital of the same size. What the CEO wanted me to do was to put out a statement and argue with the press that our actual death figures had not risen in three years. I was walking and arguing with him that it was the de facto method of measuring mortality which is accepted across the whole NHS on a fair and consistent basis, and to try to say otherwise was spin, and I didn't like it. The fact was that we were performing worse than any other NHS hospital Trust against this long-accepted method. He hung up the phone on me as he wasn't happy that I wouldn't agree. I expected to be sacked when I came in, as my predecessor had lost her job after disagreeing on a press matter.

You know the saying, 'a fish rots from the head'. Well, when it comes to organisational culture, I thoroughly agree. Remember the Fielding Review not being shared proactively? Guess what Ian Smith the Coroner at the Inquest established? Again, reported in the same article and I heard it said myself:

"Smith said he believed 11 midwives at the hospital – all of whom gave evidence at the inquest – had colluded to cover up knowledge that low temperature is a common sign of infection. He said "incriminating" notes containing observations about baby Joshua's condition may have been deliberately destroyed."

In the CEO's 'defence', I recall that he also gave evidence at the Inquest that as a former nurse, he knew that a low temperature was a sign of infection in neonates. Despite 11 of his midwives saying the contrary, I sadly have to say I've never seen anything to convince me otherwise that Joshua's notes weren't destroyed. – I'm sure I will receive some 'comments' for stating this, but when an experienced coroner and legal expert says that he believes based on all the evidence that has been given to him, that records may have been destroyed, as a member of the public, I would argue you would expect some sort of action to be taken against the staff accused by the employer. I am not a hiring and firing sort of person, but there comes a time when that is necessary, and I don't believe that you should waver.

What would I have done have after the inquest? Well, as I believed the coroner and unlike the CEO, I listened to the whole inquest as he instructed me, I'd have suspended all of the midwives involved, even if that meant the closure of the unit. The risk would have been too significant to me had I been responsible for making such a decision, as the destruction of notes is a serious safety and trust issue. So, until it was resolved, how could you let the people with this new knowledge return to work? Let me add some further context.

When I came into the Communications post in 2011, the inquest preparation was being led by the CEO. I'll be honest I didn't even know about the matter, and I was unprepared when it came around. Still, it transpires that the CEO had previously met with all of the midwives who were scheduled to give evidence at the inquest for Joshua Titcombe, along with the hospital Trust's legal advisors. They talked through possible questions essentially, and in my view, 'agreeing lines' – deliberately or not, that is what it led to. You can't really un-hear something. I accept the direct instruction may not have been given, "This is what you must say to that question," but the inference is there. I also find it odd that the CEO would personally hold such meetings rather than relying on his executive Director with portfolio responsibility to oversee and assure such matters and then for it to be delegated through the normal structure of command.

An Inquest is a judicial Inquiry. Coaching the witnesses is NOT permitted by law. A member of my team was present at these meetings, as this is what the CEO instructed and always did before 'high profile' inquests, I was later told.

A common practice for communication and media teams is to collect a Q&A document, not for publishing but as background to enable press questions to be answered expediently. It was an eye-opener when I started to work more with the media. They ask a wide range of questions each day about an organisation with around 7000 people and treating 200,000 + patients a year and expect the media officer to know about every operation and every complaint in detail – which means a preparation of notable issues is required. However, I believe it is reasonable to assume that the Q&A document was created as a record of what the witnesses would likely say if asked at the inquest, since it was based on the meeting the CEO held. Furthermore, the document was shared with the midwives by one of their senior members of department staff. This was entirely wrong, and I've stopped the practice of my team assisting a long time ago, requiring the CEO's and my authority to collate any Q&A or pre-inquest lines that could be seen and then used by a witness. We've never been asked to approve any since.

Through the release of documents following a Data Protection Subject Access Request (SAR) James Titcombe, the father of Joshua Titcombe was aware that a Q&A document had been produced and reasonably requested a copy of it. I could find no copy of this document, and therefore, wrote on behalf of the Trust to him to explain that, yet the document was mentioned in emails. One night when I was working late, I was going through old manual files, and I came across the Q&A document. I was really pleased. The next morning, I shared it with James and later that day had to speak to the coroner to explain the purpose of its production. The CEO wasn't happy with me as I didn't seek his permission to share the document. It was releasable under the Freedom of Information Act of which I was responsible for, so I undertook my duty and then briefed the CEO. Of course, there was an argument. I perhaps should have done it the other way around, but this was a document in essence about a little boy who should still be with us and come what may, I was going to do the right thing. It did cause a substantial amount of media interest. But I was sleeping better, knowing it was another piece of the jigsaw shared with the people who needed it. I'm sure the family of Joshua wanted people sacked. I would have too, but I came to realise that what they wanted above all else was the truth.

As my father had been dying, my sister Claire was very angry and looked to blame the doctors. Dad gave written consent for his records to be discussed and shared with us. We both met with his GP to query delays in diagnosis, and it was a positive experience. The GP shared her computer screen with us, and we could view and discuss all of his history leading up to the diagnosis of lung cancer, no barriers, no defensive position. It was clear his first scan as a suspected cancer patient wasn't done on time by the hospital in Southport, which, based on our other dealings with the hospital wasn't entirely a surprise. I truly believe my Trust should have taken the same approach with James and provided unrestricted access to everything, no need for requests and redactions of documentation.

I feel strongly about this and that there's a need for a 'revolution' in how patient data is managed the NHS. The clinicians and managers are merely the custodians of the patient data until such time the patient requires it. I have a vision that in the future, at some point, it will be the other way round, and it will be the patient granting access to their data to the clinicians, not the other way round.

"Please leave his room until you've found some manners."

I may have disliked my dad, but people still need to be treated with dignity and respect. I was visiting him in hospital in the weeks before his death. He was clearly dying, but the hospital wouldn't yet discharge him. I was sat in his hospital room with him. I'd just helped him go to the toilet. It was hard for me to clean and help him on the toilet. I'd do it for anyone, but to do it for someone you truly didn't like with compassion and care was tough. But I'm not a complete arse, and I did it. Afterwards, he lay in bed, reminiscing about our trip to Malaya having a laugh and a chat. A tall man with papers, smartly dressed shirt and tie and spectacles came in, followed by three younger people all dressed the same, the man and his 'ducklings' ignored me and our conversation.

"Mr Woodford," he said, standing at the side of the bed near dad and reading from his papers. He then spouted a lot of stuff about tests and that he might be able to be discharged tomorrow. "Excuse me, who are you," I interrupted. "Pardon me," said the man, now making eye contact with me as if I were one of his ducklings. Only they looked nervous. He smiled and I said, "You know the man's name in the bed, but you've barged in here while we are having a conversation and not had the respect to introduce yourself."

I smiled in return and stood up, "I am Mr Woodford's son," I said without offering my hand. Dad smiled and lay there waiting for the fight to start! "I don't need to tell anyone my name," said the man as he grew red in the face. I sat back down. The ducklings were now shuffling around, clearly, nobody had ever challenged this pompous prick before! "Dr, until you can establish your name, please leave this room until you've found some manners!"

The ducklings now looked quietly excited! The doctor turned and marched out, avoiding eye contact with me. I stood up and opened the door. He marched as the ducklings followed, "Sorry dad, but he was an arsehole, don't put up with his crap!"

"Michael has offered for me to go to a private hospital, what do you think?" Michael is my cousin and Dad's nephew, a kind man and loved my dad like his own. "We know what's next, Dad. You've had the diagnosis. I think you should just be where you'd be happiest and most comfortable, be that staying here, a private hospital or at home. Think on it tonight and tomorrow make a decision?" In the end, my brother Chris had to fight to have him discharged, delayed because of medication issues with the Doctor. I work in a hospital and understand technology and many of the challenges, so the cost of it aside I can see no reason for such issues for patients regarding medication delays.

The hospital Trust had just become the front page news following the inquest of baby Joshua Titcombe who died needlessly, following being born at one of our hospitals in Barrow. There is no good way for a parent to see their child die, but Joshua, bless him, didn't have a dignified end to his life. England's healthcare watchdog, the CQC and the NMC carried out an inspection of the hospital's maternity services.

The Nursing and Midwifery Council (NMC) is the regulator for nursing and midwifery professions in the UK. The NMC maintains a register of all nurses, midwives and specialist community public health nurses and nursing associates eligible to practise within the UK.

Now, I've signed documents as a senior manager, so I can't talk about some of the events that unfolded, but the report is available still on the CQC website. The CQC was damning in its findings, and that should have been enough, in my opinion, to make significant change happen, but it didn't. Now, there is a strange phenomenon that I've witnessed and been a part of in the NHS, and observe it time and time again. When things go wrong, the leaders go into 'hiding', literally, and believe reputation is protected through press statements. Given my 20 years' experience, I can confidently say it is a fallacy or as I'd put it, "horseshit." Reputation, be that in your personal life or in business, is about delivering your promise, not solely based on what you say. Mick and Steve at the medical transport company knew that and taught me well.

James Titcombe is Joshua's dad. I have got to know James a little bit over the years and have found he has always spoken great sense. The trust really got itself into a muddle dealing with James, as the culture got in the way each time, being defensive and uncaring. Every hospital I've ever dealt with always says it has the patient at its heart, but what I saw was when the experts were questioned, the management 'clammed up' and became obstructive, relying on solicitors to communicate with a bereaved father. I would often have Directors ask me, what did I think James and other families wanted? Other than the obvious, i.e. for people to take responsibility for their actions and to be completely open and transparent, they want the data they request – they want the truth, not as 'we' see it, but as it is. Most of my interaction with the families initially was about trying to provide them with data they had asked for either through the Freedom of Information Act, or the Data Protection Act. I realise now that they shouldn't have had to ask for any of the data. They should have been provided with all of the records and emails in a format that they could understand.

I'm not a clinician but in maternity, it's a simple 'promise'. When it is time, the person comes into the maternity unit. They are made comfortable, and a healthy baby is born and lives are changed forever. That's the promise, and that's how reputations are created. If babies die unnecessarily. Sorry doesn't even cut it. Yes, I understand that sometimes babies die, the public knows this too, but what they don't understand or accept are lies or half-truths. People are intelligent and can understand where people are involved, mistakes will happen and we know nature can be all too cruel as well as incredible. But what they (or I) don't understand or will not tolerate is it happening repeatedly. What I witnessed and I was a part of, I admit to that. You start to believe your own hype and the currency of the day is anyone who can write a report that gives you something to hide behind statements like its 'nothing we didn't already know needed to be fixed' or my other cringe-worthy example, 'there is an action plan'. Having an action plan and the report saying five babies have died is little comfort to any of the families concerned.

A pint of Guinness and steak and chips were delivered to my table. I lived about two hours away from the hospital in Barrow, and the media attention and requests were now just too great to manage in a 'normal' working day. I found myself working in the office until midnight on some occasions. I decided to stay in a local hotel, the Abbey house, rather than travel home late in the evenings and return in the dark mornings. It felt safer to stay over and be fresh if work was needed from my hotel room.

This particular morning I had been speaking to a reporter from the national newspaper The Telegraph. The reporter explained he was covering a story to do with the maternity services, and he had spoken to a family whose baby had died whilst being born at Furness General Hospital (I won't be mentioning the details here). The reporter wasn't in the area, he told me, but had some information he wanted answering quickly. He wanted to talk about the clinical circumstances of the baby's death and the mother's condition. I wouldn't have this information or access to the medical records, and nor should I. I had been robustly discussing with him that if he was speaking to the mother and the family, then he would be able to access all of this information himself through them – I was clearly calling out his bluff.

I started to drink my Guinness when two men sat down at a high table to my left, they both wore shirts and jeans and they placed their laptops on the high table whilst one of them went to the bar to order. He ordered, then returned to his stool and made a call on his mobile in a loud voice. "Yeah, I've spoken to that idiot at the hospital, what's his name, Woodford? I've told him we are not up here, and he believed it!" I still can't believe what he did next – and I regret not confronting him and telling him to show some fucking respect. In his loud unashamed voice, he began to retell over the telephone in graphic detail the traumatic birth experience of a lady and the death of her baby at birth. I couldn't believe it, they were laughing and saying what a good story it was. There was no respect at all, I agree there was (and still is) an important story to tell, but this unprofessional. I actually like the press and journalists; I admire their work and believe they are an important part of a free democratic society, but they have to do so professionally! Throughout the maternity reporting there were many articles that made for uncomfortable reading, but I can only recall two that appeared that were incorrect, one because the journalist didn't check the facts and the other because it was clearly made up and a gross exaggeration of the truth. But in the majority of cases, I'm pleased and sad to say that the reporting appeared to be accurate.

"Speak to the solicitor," my CEO instructed. It was about 9 pm at night. "We must be able to get an injunction." He protested, "It's not a good idea," I" explained, "It will cost a lot of money and how will it appear to others when they learn that you are trying to silence somebody who has lost their family?" There are many versions of this particular matter, so I will keep it brief. In around 2008, a lady died at Barrow Hospital whilst giving birth to her son; her new Born son died too. If that isn't tragic enough, her husband was also a non-clinical staff member at the hospital. A number of things happened to him over a period of months, but ultimately, he was dismissed from his employment due to ill-health. I'm sure it was all done 'by the book' at the time, as the then HR Director once told me.

I can remember asking with surprise, "What book?" I truly believe that in some situations, policies need to be torn up and people looked after. This is a hospital trust that had an annual income of around £350 million at the time. What would it have cost to let this man have a year off on full pay and helping perhaps with some counselling and specialist support, maybe £25,000? Doesn't sound a lot to me – and sounds like a simple decision to make and a good precedent to set, one based on kindness and compassion.

A staff member explained to me last year that a colleague's son was seriously ill with life-threatening cancer. They'd been treated in another part of the country, and were finding it a challenge to attend work. I offered to cover any hotel costs. I was prepared to put them on my own credit card if needed. A senior colleague said to me if I do that, I will be setting a precedent; I would have to do this for others in the future too. I thought, "It sounds like a good precedent to be setting," and I disregarded the advice.

Paying the staff member £25,000 a year to help him feel like the least the organisation could do after his wife and son died in his employer's care. So back to the injunction: the colleague who was dismissed it is a very well reported 'story'. He was looking to move to another area about 60 miles away and required references. The CEO decided to visit the colleague at his home to discuss some other matters that he had emailed the CEO about, as well as his intended move. During the meeting, the CEO offered him some money to assist with the move. I believe it was a sum of around £3000. A national newspaper had now contacted me regarding a story for the Sunday edition that would focus on the chief executive offering a bereaved ex-dismissed staff member 'hush' money to move away.

The CEO remonstrated with me, this was not the case. It was merely a human act of kindness on his part father to father. I honestly don't know any more which version I believe. Was it hush money or was it just a father in a position of power offering some support to another father? Either way, it was badly advised by the HR Director, who later claimed he knew nothing of the intention. I explained to the CEO that the facts are, "A staff member whose wife and child died in our care was also dismissed and then offered cash to 'help' him relocate away from the area." These remain the facts, however we try to justify them. The last I heard, the then CEO was trying to sue a local newspaper for defamation. After he left the trust, he called me once or twice very unhappily that I would not go on record and refute the allegation of 'hush' money. I highlighted to him on each occasion that I have no evidence as to why the money was offered. I can only state the facts as I know it and evidenced. I had written a briefing note to the regional NHS on the allegations once I became aware, but the CEO instructed me to keep it in my 'top drawer' for future use if needed…

It was needed the following week! Sunday came and again, I was sat in the dining room with my new daughter. This time, the phone rings and it is the national NHS England press office. The story had been printed, and they required an immediate briefing as the Press lead of No10 Downing Street wanted details ASAP![3]

It is important that I highlight that the CEO has always denied the allegations of making a bribe and that for him, it was merely the act of being a 'good employer'. I truly hope that this is the true version.

Never under-resource a crisis is a lesson I have learned through several situations, not least the maternity crisis. It serves no good waiting for the peak of the crisis before deciding to add capacity to a team. The peak will come, but along the way, people will become tired and sick, so it's best to not wait and to try to get ahead of the situation.

Health-wise, I hadn't been looking after myself. I was working 50 to 70 hours a week. I woke up one morning with half of my face swollen and bright red – I had some sort of infection. I took a couple of days off but received a phone

---

3 You can read the article yourself here:
https://www.dailymail.co.uk/news/article-2346554/NHS-chief-offered-bribe-hush-death-baby-Fathers-shock-scandal-hit-bosss-3-000-cash-deal.html

call from my CEO to say there is a rumour going around in the regional NHS that I couldn't cope and needed help. This made me feel insulted after everything I had given. I got in my car right away and drove to a regional NHS communications meeting in Manchester, embarrassing everybody with half of my face double the size and one eye swollen shut. Not long after, the CEO sent my wife a bouquet of flowers to say thanks for supporting me. This was nice. I was able to gather their support at the meeting to convince the trust they needed to increase capacity. I was allowed to bring in several people to assist, as well as dealing with the communications crisis. The day-to-day work still went on.

I liken the experience of the trust then akin to an old car that is being repaired and 'tuned up' at the same time. Each time a part is replaced with a new, better performing part, it puts additional pressure on another part of the car and so it starts to fail too. Eventually the whole engine goes bang – but not before the wheels fall off. It was not just maternity that quite rightly made the headlines, but we were also facing the crisis in record-keeping. I picked up the morning paper with a coffee from the hospital shop to find that a photograph of our medical records dept. had been published. Only, it looked like the records store had been burgled, however it hadn't it was just a bloody, disgraceful and disrespectful mess with records strewn everywhere. We all hit the headlines locally and nationally as it came to light that nearly 20,000 patients were forgotten about and didn't receive a follow-up outpatient appointment (including me!). I think a patient also died too, if memory serves me right.

I made myself a promise many years ago after the Kirkup Report was published that I would never be a silent witness or contributor ever again to keeping information from people.

"Mr Woodford, I've been told you can help me?"

This was about two years ago (2018). A gentleman had contacted one of our hospitals trying to get his wife's medical records updated, but came across a wall of bureaucracy around data protection. "I will do my best if I can. What can I do for you?" I asked.

"My wife, she is dying and is now unable to move and walk and is housebound. I have requested her medical records as I believe they are incorrect. We would like to correct the error please, but your rude colleagues are being obstructive and keep arguing about rules and proof of identity. I don't know what to do anymore." He was asking for a really simple thing for his wife. I can't go into details about what the correction was, but it was understandably causing him and his wife a good deal of distress. I am not using any identifiable information about him and his family, therefore, I'm going to call him John and I'm not mentioning his wife's actual illness either.

I said, "John, I understand why my colleagues have asked for the information they have, and I am sincerely sorry if they have upset you or have been rude. You are asking a very reasonable question. Can I make a suggestion please?

"Yes Mr Woodford?"

"First of all John, please call me Phil. Mr Woodford was my dad," I joked. John was now a little bit calmer. "I would need to see the paperwork and your identity. No disrespect intended, but just based on a phone call I don't actually have any evidence as to who you are or that your wife has consented to these changes." He was keenly listening. I continued, "Let me make a suggestion. You don't live very far away, how about I get in the car and come for a cup of tea with you now and I can collect the documentation and work on the amendments, and if your wife is able to, I could speak to her for her consent? How does that sound?" I actually can't change anyone's records, but I felt he didn't need to know that. I was sure I could find someone who could help if needed though.

"Phil, I can't believe that someone in your position is offering to come and do that."

"John, it's my job to make sure that you and your wife get what you need. To put it bluntly, you pay my wages!"

"Thank you. And yes, that would be great, please come around. I will put the kettle on and will see you in one hour." It was already about 4 pm and getting dark. I am quite sure there were some rules that I was breaking in going around to his house and was also perhaps putting myself at risk. But this was the compassionate thing to do for him and his wife to put them at ease.

I arrived at about 6 pm after getting a little bit lost with the satnav. "Coming, Phil. It's lovely to see you," he said gripping my hand and shaking it at the door. I met his wife. It was quite difficult she really wasn't well.

We sat in the kitchen John and I, drinking tea and eating biscuits. "Have you had an accident Phil? You walk with a walking stick, if you don't mind me asking?"

"I don't mind at all John," but to be honest, it seemed a little insignificant at that moment. I went on to tell him briefly about the stroke and got the usual response, "but you're too young for that." "Tell me about it. Right, let's look at this documentation and see what I can do. Yes, I can see what the problem is. I will need to speak to your GP and see if we can correct this."

John smiled then disappeared. My mind got carried away and I was looking for exits quickly in case he was about to reappear with an axe! John came back and placed a gift that he had made for me. He also had another in a box. "Philip, I'm a craftsman and I make these things to sell. I would love to give this to you as a gift for your desk, but I also have another. I spoke to your secretary and you've taught her well. She was really polite and kind when I first rang up, unlike your other colleagues. Please give this one to her with my thanks." I have to name the 'secretary', it was my PA at the time, Cara. I haven't taught her anything, she's just a great, great person, who cares – thanks Cara, whatever your role in a hospital, we can all make a difference I believe.

"I will, John. It's very kind of you and although unnecessary, I won't insult you by refusing the gift. I have to be honest, John. I'm really worried about you, you understandably look tired and frustrated. What support are you getting?"

He looked a little uncomfortable, and in typical man style not wanting to talk about his own feelings. "I don't need any help, Phil. It is my wife who needs the help." He replied with a bit of desperation in his voice. "John, I can't ignore what I've seen and heard. I won't go behind your back but to let you know when I speak to your GP, I am going to ask them to call you and see what additional support they can assist with. I also note that your wife is now disabled. I am happy to help even in the evenings if you need with any with filling out the disability claim forms so that you can claim for Personal Independence Payments. As I've had to go through this myself, I know it can be quite stressful on your own. I will also post you details of your local citizens' advice (CAB) who can also provide you with some information, if you don't mind?"

"Phil, this is very kind. We are finding it difficult to manage financially, and I am having to finish work so that I can be her full-time carer. I would welcome your help."

All this time I was talking to him, James and his son Joshua were on my mind. I have made a promise to myself that I will go the extra mile and break the 'rules' if needed to make sure people got the information they needed. I've dealt with many complaints from customers and patients in different jobs over the years and quite enjoy it. At the end of the day, they often don't want what you think they do. Most of the times, they want someone to listen and believe them and do something about it. But I have often found that people being people think the worst of others. I don't think I did anything particularly special for John, but yes, we did get the medical records updated and his GP agreed to contact and provided the support John needed.

Chapter 13: Prime Minister

Sorting my emails one Friday night before heading home, I saw that one was from 10 Downing Street. I read the email, which didn't have a lot of details, but it said I was invited to meet Theresa May, the Prime Minister at No10 for a reception! I'm a lad from a Council Estate (The Projects if you're stateside); to me, a reception is the bit you see as you enter a building. My head was now spinning, imagine if this was real?

I waited until Monday, and I telephoned Downing Street and it turned out the email was genuine! I can't even recall how I got the phone number, guess it was on the invite! I have to telephone Parliament occasionally, as part of my job, so I wasn't particularly nervous – they too are just people. I had reasoned with myself that it was probably some sort of phishing scam. It later transpired that an MP had put my name forward to represent the local NHS and meet the Prime Minister at a celebration of the NHS's 70th birthday.

I feel I've worked hard in my career to create good relationships. I believe in what is called "playing a straight bat" whenever possible; no bullshit or spin, just be kind and tell it how it is. Not everyone likes this attitude as it creates a lot of angst for others; "Phil, you're going to say what?" is the usual incredulous response. But you know what, I've learned that I'd rather be criticised for being open and honest, than being a liar or a person who hides the truth. I know I have to work on my 'tone' at times and the sarcastic laden scouse intonation!

Above all, I hate fellow communication and PR practitioners who can't answer a fucking question in a straight way. Tell the boss "No!" when they want to spin the truth. It's our job to protect and help them too.

I wore my best suit. I'd only bought it the year before for our wedding in New York, but then I had worn it with Converse Chuck Taylors. We had gotten married on a street corner underneath Manhattan Bridge! This time though, I was in my black leather work shoes, limping up to the gates of Downing Street. I felt anxious as I walked proudly past the throng of tourists snapping their pictures of me, and me trying to act 'cool' in my RayBan wayfarers and dark suit. I handed the armed police officer at the security station my invite and passport and after the security checks, walked through into Downing Street.

It was a lovely warm Autumn evening, no breeze. I even saw the cat that lives at No 10! There was a black Range Rover with dark windows and the driver's door was open. I walked past it, peering in. There was a man sat in the seat; we smiled at each other.

"Hello Sajid!" I said as though the then Home Secretary and I were best buddies.

I walked up until I was opposite No 10, conscious of my limp and worried that I'd slip on my way in, as I was still a little unsteady at times. A smartly dressed gentleman of about 60 with greying hair showed me in through the door and asked for my mobile phone. This was placed into a rack on the left. I looked around the huge, but not overly grand entrance area and a lady then escorted me down a hallway to a stairway on my right. 'Do I ask if there is an elevator, I thought?' I hate asking that as people always look at me like 'what a fat lazy man'. I wished I'd used my walking stick – it always stops the accusatory and dismissive looks when I need a little bit of assistance. I hobbled up the massive staircase feeling nervous and proud at the same time.

It was quiet. I was shown into an enormous room where I was offered drinks and snacks by waiters with trays. I took an orange juice and the smallest sandwich known to man. A hand gripped my shoulder. It was an MPs and his fiancé. "Phil, we wondered if you were coming as we didn't receive any confirmation after we put your name forward to attend!"

I explained that I was never told how I came to be invited. I agreed I'd stay to hear the speeches from Jeremy Hunt and the PM, then head over to the bar in Parliament for a drink next to the Thames and then maybe to go and grab a meal somewhere. I was shown a large, impressive room where the PM's cabinet would meet – this felt great! I thought it was nice to see all of this and with friends, what an absolute fucking honour.

No10 is like the Tardis from Dr Who; inside there must have been over 100 people in the main room on the first floor. Once you go in through the front door, there is no old welsh dresser-cum-sideboard with drawers stuffed full of shit like used batteries or takeout menus and pens. Instead, there is a collection of boxes, the mail sorting type pigeon holes which are all numbered and you deposit your mobile phone in one. I can't recall if you get some sort of token to collect it later – I think it was more like an 'honesty'-based system. I used the toilet near the entrance mainly because the ladies at work wanted me to bring a 'memento' back (steal!). I thought they would have some lovely posh hand soap, but they didn't! Not even embossed toilet paper, how very un-trusting!

I decided to go on a bit of wander and look around! I wandered back out of the main room and ended up standing at a main grand carpeted staircase about four steps from the top. I was studying the pictures of past PMs when the Prime

Minister, Theresa May, whizzed past really fast with her important looking entourage heading downstairs. About 10 minutes later she came back up the stairs, a bit more calmly this time. Perhaps she was just desperate for a poop and was now heading back as the host, dressed in a smart fitted blue suit – how very corporate to wear blue and 'on brand!' I thought.

She stopped and smiled at me as I stood there. I was still a little unsteady on my feet. I must have looked it. A waiter walked past at the top of the stairs, carrying a tray of drinks. He stopped as he saw the PM, as though this was the rule. She offered me a glass of wine, I said, "Yes please." I'd given up drinking alcohol by this point, but it's the PM who's offering! It felt wrong to say "no," and I was enjoying being next to her. I remembered quickly a story a colleague told me where he'd been in a meeting in No10 and he'd told the PM of the time to "Fuck off!!" for not taking his medical advice! I wondered if I could top that story?

Theresa May had a great bum I thought. This was bad of me – a playful slap on the arse, perhaps? Hmmm, that went horribly wrong in primary school with a girl, but this was a whole different level of bragging rights. Could I be put in the Tower of London for slapping her arse? I pictured SAS operatives jumping on me if I touched her – so I didn't! But I did laugh to myself at the thought. We exchanged some small talk about the Prime Ministers that had walked on these stairs and then she disappeared back into the crowd. I went back into the room where I met a colleague who introduced me to Jeremy Hunt, the then Secretary of State for Health. I'd met him several times before and always liked him. The last time I'd last met him was at work on 16 June 2016. I remember it well, sadly, as it was the awful day that Jo Cox the Labour MP was shot, stabbed, and murdered in Birstall, West Yorkshire.

I clearly had made an impression as he introduced me to the crowd around him as Paul! I've been called a lot worse, so I didn't correct him. Last time we'd met, Jeremy had met with a group of our clinicians for a private but open chat. I'd stood outside the room with his staff as the news flashed up on my mobile – awful thing to happen to anyone, but this felt like an assault on our democracy to me. That day, I was showing Jeremy around the hospital. A Junior Doctor came up to me and said, "I see he's ignoring the doctors (there was a lot of bad feeling towards him at the time from doctors across the country). "I'd tell him to fuck off if he spoke to me," said the Jnr Doc. I offered to introduce him to Jeremy if he'd like to tell him to his face! But of course he was all talk, and declined. The next day, the local newspaper ran a story by a doctor's union that Jeremy Hunt refused to speak to doctors due to the National pay dispute. It was a fabrication, a blatant lie. I saw him introduce himself to doctors at every chance. He was clearly very skilled at it. As we approached about 5 doctors in the Emergency Department, he stepped forward and stood amongst them making jokes and putting them all at ease.

That's it, no other stories about the PM! And no scandals or arse slapping!

Decades earlier, I had met and driven the Prime Minister of Morocco. I was a General Manager for an ambulance service, and he was visiting to view some specialist rescue equipment, and as I was the only manager there with a vaguely smart car, A BMW coupe and with an advanced driving test pass, I was 'chosen' to drive him to the train station. We chatted about football and the Morocco footballers who had played for Coventry City, Haji and Youssef as I dropped him off at the station. I checked his ticket, it was standard class. He told me a story about how he had spoken with President Bush on agreeing to join the war on terror – this was not long after 9/11. It was great making small talk with such an important person. He was very down to earth though and recalled his trips to Anfield to watch Liverpool FC in the 1970s. a golden era for the club indeed. Before I walked him to the train carriage at Preston Station I arranged and paid for his ticket to be upgraded to first class, I was no martyr I claimed this extra cost back!

Chapter 14: Motorcycles and Travel

Motorcycles have played a significant part in my life. I've toured Spain, France and Germany on motorbikes, mostly in groups. I started riding a motorbike when I joined college straight from school as a form of commuting, and then after I was divorced from Kate; call it a midlife crisis, I don't know? I first bought the sports car, but also passed my motorcycle riding test and went straight out and purchased a 1000 CC motorcycle, much to the worry of everybody, but me. When you buy a car, people don't come along telling you you're going to die, but strangely when you buy a motorcycle the first thing you find is that people seem to enjoy eroding your confidence by recounting stories of somebody they knew who had died in a motorcycle accident. – Why? I don't want that in my head when I'm riding, piss off!

I am mad about motorcycles. I think it is a combination of things, the power, the freedom, a little bit of the speed, and the noise, but also the smell of the engine and hot oil. It is all quite evocative. I've never been a fast rider or overly confident. I gave up and sold my last motorcycle not long after we adopted our children as I had less time to devote to riding between cafes eating bacon sandwiches and drinking coffee. My wife Shana passed her motorcycle test about a year or two after me so that she could participate in something with me. This was really kind of her, but I found it immensely difficult. I would spend most of my time following her, worried that she was going to crash. It was like I was a father figure rather than a friend and partner, sexist I know, but that was honestly how I felt, very protective.

Germany – "Let's all agree – nobody mentions the war," I thought about these words as I hunkered down behind the fairing on the autobahn heading towards the Rhineland in Germany. I was never an overly confident motorbike rider, but here I am on a 170bhp BMW sports tourer, powering on with 20 riders I don't know. I was overtaken by a young lad on a Suzuki SV650, but he wasn't sitting on the seat – he was stood on it, squatting with one-hand on the throttle, his left hand waving across to me! "Fucking maniac," I said out loud into my helmet! He really worried me. I could feel my legs turn to jelly a little bit. Was I going to need my first aid skills shortly? Unlikely, as at this speed, we would be likely be using a hosepipe and brush to get his body off the tarmac. There would be no resuscitation. We all knew the risks involved in riding, particularly in a group and at high speed, and there are some unwritten rules about not putting your fellow riders in jeopardy. I rolled off the throttle and dropped to the back of the line of bikes. This was my second big bike trip abroad. I was now in the 'tail-end-Charlie' position, the rule is the first rider waits at each turning until the last person, the tail-end-charley' comes through and then the person who waited catches up and drops into the group, lots of variations happen with this system, but this is the basic idea.

Spain – my first time riding abroad was with two mates, one of whom was Tim. A different bike a year earlier than Germany, but I was equally unconfident that time, riding across northern Spain to Barcelona. We kicked back in the sun, enjoying a beer, espresso and tapas near Plaça Catalunya as a moped rider was T-boned by a car at a junction. He flew like a rag doll up in the air. We didn't help we were on our highest level of suspicion and guard, trying not to act like a tourist.' Some other people rushed over and helped, but we were seriously worried that it was a staged incident either for insurance or for people to leave what they were doing and come over – drastic, I know, and I absolutely love Barcelona and Spain, but in our research we had been warned about scams and thefts in Barcelona. He walked away and got into a taxi, maybe we were right to be suspicious?

Germany – settling into our hotel in a small town in Germany was exciting. We all ended up in the bar. I got my pint of beer and sat down. A few locals were at the bar. Three men said "Hallo" to us all, then they started to discuss the war! "I see you are all invading our small town on your motorbikes just like you tried back in the 1940s!" They smiled and patted each other on the back, laughing. We all laughed; in that moment we knew it was going to be a good holiday. They were just like us; they broke the ice and shared beer or five with us!

I love how travelling brings so many adventures, many of which you can't plan. That's serendipity, and it's the best thing for adventures, in my opinion:

San Francisco – we walked around the corner, my first wife and the in-laws. A huge man in a doorway was stood staring and said, "What are you doing on my block?" He snarled with intent. We ignored him and continued walking. We were all seasoned travelers, particularly in North America, but then something strange happened. After a few yards, a hulk of a man looking like he was a gangster from Starsky and hutch stepped out from between two car wrecks, wearing a pink suit and shiny black shirt and oddly a baseball hat. He was clutching his penis through his pants, walking towards us; we thought, 'Fuck this is bad!' Or maybe only I thought that to myself. I'm not sure everybody else saw him in the same way I did as nobody said anything. He took his penis out and waved it towards us, mumbling something. We continued to walk.

We didn't discuss this incident at the time, but I think we knew if we stopped, it wasn't a conversation he wanted. We were in San Francisco. I don't remember it being like South

Central LA in Mrs. Doubtfire! We turned right at the next block corner and found the restaurant at the top we were searching for. We were only a couple of blocks from the famous Union Square area. It was two blocks across on the left corner, so being tourists, we thought we could just go around the block! Whilst we were relatively savvy travelers, we weren't aware that San Francisco, so close to the city center, would be like this; perhaps it was just a blip? We hadn't researched the city; we had jumped on the first available flight we could afford using Kate's parents'' airline discounts. Our knowledge of the City was TV shows in which the city always looked friendly and safe a bit hippy-like 'full of love'; in fairness the rest of it probably was. I'd go back without hesitation. Kate's mum worked for Canadian Airlines at the time. A perk of employment was discounted or free Air travel, based on seniority and length of service. After the meal, the waiter warned us we weren't in a tourist area and shouldn't walk back to our hotel! We left the restaurant and pushed past the prostitutes, and got into a waiting cab the waiter had kindly arranged for us. The taxi driver was equally surprised to hear that we had walked there and was unsurprised when we relayed the story to him!

We went to a bar near our hotel. A few beers later, the parent in-laws made their way alone back to the hotel. We had another drink and watched some crazy American sport on the TV in the bar. We strolled back through Union

Square, past the mounds of homeless people and to our hotel. We opened the hotel door, knowing something was not quite right, only to find wife's dad on top of her mum getting 'jiggy'. We ran down the corridor laughing embarrassingly, uncontrollably! Not sure now where we were going as we were all sharing a room to save money. We eventually plucked up the courage and went back – her dad looked as proud as punch and gave me a can of beer. He said, "I'm glad you didn't come in 5 minutes earlier!" He said it proudly like a stud with his chest puffed out. Still in his underpants! However Kate's mum, was in the bathroom, sat on the floor in her nightdress, crying!

Spain and France – from Barcelona, we rode north to France, Perpignan and Narbonne. I had an incredible ride over the Pyrenees. The Pyrenees were beautiful, but I enjoyed the coast ride from Barcelona to the mountains the most, darting up and down the Cliffside roads and down into tourist towns with lovely beaches and the sun burning down. It felt great to be alive. I fell ill in Narbonne. My arthritis was flaring up badly. There was a terrible pain in my right hand, causing it to feel like it was on fire and with 'pins and needles'. It later transpired I had developed Carpal Tunnel syndrome.4 I required surgery to correct. Not long after

---

4 According to the NHS: Carpal tunnel syndrome (CTS) is pressure on a nerve in your wrist. It causes tingling, numbness and pain in your hand and fingers. You can often treat it yourself, but it can take months to get better.

returning home I was struggling to hold onto the handlebars and was getting cramp and pains in the arches of my left foot, which was hindering me from changing gears. I agreed I'd meet the lads at the Eurotunnel in northern France in a week, but I needed to rest and was to make my way North on my own. They both rode off to the northeast to Austria and Germany with the Nürburgring racetrack as their prize.

After a couple of days of pain riding and walking around historic Narbonne, going from bar to bar, I sorted an auto train to Paris on the Auto-train, I found it difficult to book the ticket, but a few local people walking past helped me out. The vehicle, my motorbike went on one train and the people went in a separate passenger carriage.

I woke up the following day even stiffer and in pain from sleeping to Paris in a reclining chair. I rode out of Paris Bercy station into the traffic chaos of Paris. Paris is a magical place, and even the traffic chaos is stylish with the backdrop of Parisian architecture. I was lost, for the first time on a trip! GPS was only for the rich, and iPhones were not yet a thing that everybody could afford, and I had no plan, no map and no grasp of the language other than being able to order a beer and a cheese and ham sandwich! Oh and I could say left and right and ask where the police station is, just all the non-essential stuff I learnt at school.

I was lost so I pulled the bike over. I was riding a huge 1000cc KTM adventure touring monster. I sat on a bench, head in my hands. "Hey mate, you ok?" boomed a cockney accent from behind a helmet of a biker atop a black Ducati. I was soon to find out he was heading home to Croydon in Surrey and offered to let me follow him through Paris all the way to the Eurotunnel. We set off.

I felt some trepidation at following some stranger across an equally strange city, but in all my travels I have found that people are generally very helpful. I kept this outlook and did my best to keep up with him. He was great at the city riding but he didn't know I was a shit rider with 'all the gear and no idea.' I soon adjusted to the aggressive 'point and squirt' style of riding needed in Paris, using the brakes hard and accelerating fast, away from junctions and into the tiny gaps in the traffic. With the huge touring panniers, it wasn't straightforward, but it was bloody good fun! I was singing loudly in my helmet most of the time! I started to enjoy myself and got used to being beeped as I darted in and out, making the bike back fire as I rolled off the throttle, and stopping quickly at traffic lights. We said goodbye over a coffee and a cheese-toasted sandwich at a service station outside of Paris. I quite like riding alone, though!

I had a few days till the lads would turn up to meet me as I had made good time using the auto train to skip across France, and I was now feeling like the king of the world and a bit overconfident. So with no map but a picture in my mind of where the main points in the country were, I headed to Normandy to see the D-Day landing sights. I first visited Pegasus Bridge, the famous location from Operation Overlord, where I met a lady telling stories to tourists about her memory of WWII and her watching it all unfold, she was a young child when the allied gliders coming in at night! She told us.

She talked of being a little girl no more than six in her nightgown looking out of the bedroom window as she witnessed the silent gliders make their descent into northern France. She was describing with emotion the night of 5th June, 1944. A force of 181 men, led by Major John Howard, took off from RAF Tarrant Rushton in Dorset, southern England in six Horsa gliders to capture Pegasus Bridge, and also 'Horsa Bridge', a few hundred yards to the east, over the Orne River. Sat in a cafe next to the bridge, with all the tourists clutching their hot coffee, other than her voice and that of the translator, the only other sound you could hear were the gulps of people as we forgot to even breathe as we listened to her story. There wasn't a dry eye amongst us. Me the dirty looking biker, helmet in one hand and a coffee in the other, crying into my cup!

The next few days, I toured all the D-Day landing sights, chatting with locals about my ability to say left and right and drinking beer and ordering cheese and ham sandwiches. I had grown up hearing mixed things about the French being rude and hostile. I assume an outdated legacy and myth of WWII, but what I encountered were friendly and hospitable people proud of their country and history and the ability to make fantastic food. Thankfully, I never did need to ask where the police station was!

A few days later, I met the lads at the Eurotunnel at a shopping mall – they'd had a blast, literally. They made me feel jealous with all their boasting of racing around the Nürburgring! I took it all with a 'pinch of salt' 'about how they'd sped around the 'Nürburgring a bit like tall stories from fishermen. We stayed together until we all reached the M25 and what felt like the country's longest traffic jam. I swear I was stuck in slow traffic for the 500 miles home! We split up as I showed off my new Paris bike riding skills!

Except the horns were now replaced with shouts of "wanker!" Not as friendly as Paris. The French had certainly been much more polite with their remonstrating in traffic!

The Netherlands – I started to feel sick I'd 'lost' my fiancé in Holland! Four of us had set off the day before from Burnley, and my mate was on his Honda Sports bike (Blade) with his wife perched on the back. Shana and I were on our bikes. Next stop, the Dutch MotoGP in Assen, Netherlands, to see my racing idol – Valentino Rossi! We got split up on our way back from the race to our hotel. It was an incredible experience. There must have been at least 10,000 motorbikes all exiting the circuit at the same time, with the Dutch motorway lined with locals waving and cheering. I wish I knew how to wheelie! I had to pull over as I developed a fuel leak! Once it was all sorted, thanks to a Dutch police officer assisting, we sped off, but my fiancé was a bit too quick for me, and we quickly became split up in the traffic chaos. A few hours later, she came across a Dutch couple who helped direct her to the hotel. You always worry on a bike about others when you can't see them; the 'what ifs' pop into your mind.

Germany – I did make it to the Nürburgring with the twenty lads. I probably hold the lap record for the slowest lap ever! But it was great fun. I don't have any tall tales of how I went round the 70+ bends/corners scraping my knee as each attempt. I certainly did have one or two moments where my heart was in my mouth, and I felt my knee touch the tarmac. It is Nirvana for sports bike riders and brings with it maximum bragging rights.

I had been having a brew with a colleague at work in the college I worked at. Julie was new, and we were getting to know each other and I told her I rode a motorbike. She then explained about her husband going to Germany tomorrow with 19 others and said a space was available. I knocked on my boss's door, and he agreed I could take the next two weeks off as annual leave. I then telephoned my actual boss, my fiancé Shana. Then in less than 24 hours, I was on the motorway with Julie's husband, John. We were heading for Hull to catch the overnight ferry to Rotterdam with John's son riding a new sporty Suzuki 650. In two days, he would become the crazy biker seat surfing next to me on the autobahn!

Malaya – on another travel journey (not motorcycles sadly – but we did see Valentino Rossi!), my brother at 6'2" and me at 5'10" found ourselves stick out on the streets of Kuala Lumpur, where most locals were much shorter. We stood out, especially as I have a large tattoo on my right forearm and they are not very common in the country. We boarded a monorail, making our way with some difficulty through the daily commuting home crowd and boarded the train. Chris was jostled as he boarded, knocking into a young girl of no more than ten years of age. Five minutes later, he realized it wasn't just a jostle, he'd had his pocket picked and his phone was gone. I shouldn't laugh, but Chris is a big man, an ex-soldier and is involved in security now for a living. The irony wasn't lost on the family when we re-grouped!

San Francisco – yet another experience took place in San Francisco. I'd never seen so many homeless people in one place. I spent time chatting with a homeless man and sharing a Starbucks coffee with him. He told me that there are so many homeless people in the city due to mild weather and a wealthy population. On this particular day of the trip, I was hunting down a golf shop. My mate back home had asked me to buy him a specific golf putter made by the golf equipment manufacturer Titleist. The particular club was a Scotty Cameron putter, very cheap in the states he said. I had taken a list of several golf shops in San Francisco with me on the holiday. Phoning one of them the day before from the hotel, I found the club cost $130, and they had put it aside for me. I got pushed around with Kate as we boarded the bus, then got into an argument with a homeless person asking me for money. "No, I'm sorry I don't have any spare money to give you," I said. "Just a few bucks," he pleaded. As I stood at the bus stop, he grabbed at me. I reacted, and a very minor scuffle happened – embarrassing, but I lost $130 in the process as either the homeless person or someone else helped themselves to my golf club money in my pockets! My mate never did believe me when I got home, I think he thought I had forgotten to try to buy it!

Vancouver - yet another experience, this time in beautiful Canada my 'spiritual' home in North Vancouver. My mate and I entered a coffee shop, When the Manager came over to us and said, "I'm sorry, we're filming a Chuck Norris Movie here you can't leave the café, but you can stay and have a free coffee if you'd like, but you will need to wait about an hour or so before you can leave?" so, we sat down and waited! We had been hunting out a shop that sold specialist 'War Craft games'. My mate was madly into these games and, on this side of the city, there was a famous gaming shop. While this was hugely exciting, we never saw much. However, as it all happened very slowly, we noticed a big American car fly past and then there he was, Chuck at the top of the street. I was 100ft away from someone who had known Bruce Lee and Steve McQueen! Unreal; there's nothing else to say about that day, but I did see two bears in the wild on that trip! I idolized both stars as a young kid and still do, so this felt special and surreal as I had read a fair bit about Chuck Norris and his Karate background.

These are all memories that I think about quite frequently. I want to take Shana and the girls there one day to see British Columbia. I think they will love it too, especially the mountains. I haven't been able to write about everywhere I've been. I have a dream and a strong desire for my daughters to travel as soon as possible, with or without us both!

My dream remains to retire either in Netherlands or Canada and ride my bicycle all day long – just maybe?

Chapter 15: Dead or Alive?

How would you end your life?

I had already investigated assisted dying and Dignities whilst I was in the hospital. But as I was unable to walk, it was unlikely that I could get myself to Switzerland. I'm not sure how I would have my life end. It was hard to research how to kill yourself on a mobile phone with only one working arm and hand and constantly crying and hallucinating. This was a terrifying period for me and still haunts me.

I've had a view before about people who take their own life I didn't think them selfish or brave, it was just something I could understand without judgement. In my case, the feeling has come over me maybe three or four times in my life. First, when Spot had been killed; second, whilst I was in the hospital following the stroke; and soon after being discharged, thirdly and most recently, following a berating by a colleague at work. I have reflected on them many times and conclude that on each occasion, I had lost the feeling of having a sense of purpose in the world, and without a purpose, I genuinely believe we have nothing.

I was sitting in the conservatory at home and now needed a stick to assist me to walk. I had Vale, my dog and best friend lying next to me. "It's ok, Dad. I'll look after you," he said through his eyes. "Thanks, son." Tears dripped down my face as I told him. My Fiancé had gone to work, and through my self-pitying mind, I struggled to see any future or any worth left in my life. Sure, there are people much worse off, but that didn't make me feel any better.

The care workers would be visiting me at 12 to help make my lunch and then the physiotherapist Tamsin would arrive from the hospital. "This is no life, Vale." I'm sorry, mate, I'm going." Vale knew what I meant. I weighed-up my options in my puddled mind.

Hanging – how? I can't stand up!

Wrists – that seemed too painful. I'd been there before, nope.

Overdose…? Hmm, I've seen that go wrong for a friend.

Hanging it was. I would use the chair I was sat on, buy a rope from Amazon, and even with one good arm, I felt I could go through with it, throwing the rope over the bracing bar of the conservatory ceiling. I could make a noose with one hand. I'd practiced it with a shoelace, and it couldn't be much harder with the rope, could it?

Tamsin was a great support, and I looked forward to her visits; stroke care focuses a lot on hospital care, but that's a tiny part in most survivors lives, though a crucial one. We need greater focus, energy and investment in the community and mental health care, as it is in the community where we hope to spend the rest of our lives, not in a hospital. Thank you to Tamsin and her colleagues for putting up with me and my depression; you were all great getting me walking again. Several years later, Tamsin would assist me in walking up the tallest mountain in England: Scafell Pike, I didn't quite make it, but my friends and Tamsin left me with a treasured new memory.

I googled all of the medications I had, nothing definitive appearing around overdoses. However, I knew someone who once tried paracetamol but ended up in a worse situation, needing a kidney transplant. I telephoned the conservatory company. "Hi. I want to mount a TV in the Conservatory. Can you tell me how much weight the ceiling strut will take?"

"Let me check on that. Do you know what the TV weight is?" the call-taker replied. I said, "I haven't a clue. I'm not very good with kilograms, but I think it would be about 100 Kg with the brackets and wiring, maybe?"

"That's very heavy. I will just check." The representative returned and said, "I've spoken with our technical support, and they have advised not to hang anything from the strut as if it broke, the ceiling could collapse!"

After the call, I thought, 'Bloody hell, I can see this going wrong. Being found underneath a glass ceiling, I would be in a worse position than I was before.'

Quite clearly, I didn't act upon it. Instead, I spoke to a support worker from the charity The Stroke Association. Sally Farnell (real name) came out to visit me at home the same day. We sat at the table and had a drink. Sally listened whilst I constantly cried like a child. She never passed judgement; she took the time to listen. She explained how I was grieving for what I felt I had lost, and she drew me a diagram illustrating it. I can no longer recall the detail of the illustration, but it felt like a lightbulb moment! I could now see why I felt like I did and perhaps what I needed to do in order to feel better. The tears stopped for the rest of the day.

About six months later, the local May Day parade took place in my town, something we've attended every year as my kids have always taken part in it. This year was different. I hobbled out of the house using my walking stick or, as I call it, my 'sympathy stick'. People don't question why I sat in the disabled seat on a bus or train. The stick acts as a sort of passport, and it's just how it is.

I made it to the main road. What typically took me 60 seconds now took 10 minutes of painful hobbling. Me, my fiancé and daughters and their grandma were together. It was busy near the road as the May Day 'floats' went by with children from the local schools and sports groups on them in various costumes. We stood on the pavement amongst the crowd. "I wish people would move," said a man with a strong accent. He had two children next to him. He was unhappy about how busy it was. Finally, he decided to move, and I felt him push me as he went past. My blood boiled, and my heart rate quickened. All you had to do was say, "Excuse me," I said to him after he had pushed past. He spun round, "What did you say? I was here first; you lot came along blocking my view!"

I felt the anger build up inside of me. I had never felt this in a long time, not like this. It was rage, not just anger, but a monstrous uncontrollable rage, and I was frightened of myself. 'Fuck you,' I thought. "I'm not taking this shit in front of my family," I replied aggressively. "Do that again, and I'll wrap this fucking walking stick around your neck," I threatened him as menacingly as a disabled person can, wielding a hospital-issued metal walking stick.

I knew in my mind how to defend myself from a decade of martial arts as a teenager, but I suddenly realized how vulnerable I was; I was shaking. We continued to exchange threats until my youngest daughter grabbed my sleeve, saying, "Dad, dad!" I could see she was frightened, but I wasn't able to pull back from my position. Then, finally, I heard another man say, "Come on, let it go. There are children here." I instantly knew he was right, but I was angry at myself. I wanted to vomit; and then we went home. I now study and attend self-defense classes using the martial art iKrav Maga from Israel, and it feels like a much more practical 'system' to me, less 'showy' than, say, oriental fighting styles. My youngest daughter (11) attends with me; she loves the opportunity to put on the boxing gloves and hit me a bit too much, I think! I'm planning on building a home training gym shortly in my garage so I can work out most days.

The next day, I went to see my doctor, explained what had happened, and I needed some help. He agreed. I was already taking anti-depressants medication. He referred me to the local mental health provider, requesting psychiatric intervention. It took several weeks, but in the end, the doctor received a written reply, which he discussed with me. "I'm sorry, Philip, they have declined to assess you. They have advised me to increase your medication."

"But how do they know that is the right thing to do if they don't see me?" I queried. "I know it isn't a good position with regards to mental health services in the area. I am sorry," said the doctor. I agreed for the medication to be increased and then went home and contacted a private mental health care provider. "Can you help me, please? I'm at the end of my rope and feel like I am going to harm somebody if not myself. I need help, please?" The lady answering the call wrote down everything and then said somebody would get back to me later that week.

I felt despondent again, and I didn't think I could wait another week. I, however, got a phone call back from them in less than an hour. "I've spoken to one of our neuropsychologists, Sarah, and she would be pleased to see you." I made an appointment for the following week, and she asked if my fiancé, Shana, would also come along. The next week, we went to the appointment. I felt so relieved at the end that I wasn't going mad. Sarah was one step ahead of me, fully understanding my feelings and emotions and why I felt like I did. She had also spoken with Shana separately, which I was pleased about – not the separate bit, just that somebody was also looking out for her. Caroline gave me some immediate strategies, which I try to use today still to cope better. I saw Sarah on and off in a private capacity each week for the next two months. I was lucky to be able to afford the treatment that cost around £150 a session. I feel for those people that aren't as fortunate as me.

At the end of the two months, I was having no more suicidal thoughts. My anger was now under control too. We had concentrated on me dealing with acceptance. At first, I struggled with the notion that I hadn't accepted what happened to me, but clearly, I hadn't, and was fighting it constantly. This is no longer the case. Things are tough, and I am always tired and fatigued at the extra effort both mentally and physically to carry out what were once simple, everyday tasks, but instead, I now look as to how I can make these once-simple tasks less of an effort, not just for me but also for my family and those around me.

Chapter 16: Vale

Vale was a Weimaraner and my best friend, he still is, I have him in a box next to me now as I type this. I named him Vale after the motorcyclist Valentino Rossi, who was nicknamed Vale (valley), and also because Vale was born in Wales. So Vale/Valley seemed apt too.

Every dog owner has that unique gift of being able to hold a conversation with their dog in a way that only they both can understand.

"What would you like to talk about Philip?" Asked the counsellor. I was more interested in her breasts than talking! But I was here to talk, and this wasn't going to be an hour-long excerpt from a graphic adult novel. Even if it was, I was not in a fit state for romance or sex! 'Anything'. Hmm I considered the question. I think about killing myself most days, but if I said that, I'd have to talk about it, and I didn't want to. Depression is a vicious circle; talking can hurt and not talking can make it worse.

"I can't tell you what to say, and I can't give you advice. We will just see where the conversation takes us!" 'It doesn't sound much like a good conversation to me,' I thought. This isn't what I was expecting. I thought there'd be some questions, probing into if I had daddy issues! If I mention killing myself, I thought this would get complicated. I'll be referred to a special team who will want to examine if I'm going to do it or am just thinking about it, and that sounded too tiring to me. Do people who want to kill themselves tell people? As surely they know they'll attempt to stop them, and then where does that then leave the poor soul?

"Did you see last night's Champions League game?" The look on her face indicated that clearly, you couldn't talk about whatever you wanted. So, I said, "I see my dog everywhere. When I'm at work, riding my bike, he's often there and talking to me."

"That's nice. A lot of dog owners talk to their dogs," she replied. "I know, but mine has been dead for a year and for the last 10 minutes, he's had his head in your lap!" She just smiled! Clearly my jokes weren't going to cut it with her. Fuck, I'm going to have to talk about why I speak to a dead dog now. I don't want to stop seeing or hearing him, I like it.

I do see him everywhere, and I don't want it to change. I know he's dead; I was there sat on the floor with him when the vet put the rainbow bridge medicine into him. The cancer had eaten away at him, but he looked so peaceful as he drifted off. He sits in the car with me on my daily 75-mile round trip commute and in meetings, saying, "They are talking shit again, dad!" He doesn't appear to pay compliments! I was clearing some space in the garage recently and I came across his old car blankets – essentially a dirty old duvet cover. It was unwashed; I put it to my face and breathed in. It was delightful. Proust described the olfactory phenomenon in Remembrance of Things Past, the feelings of 10 happy years alive together came flooding back to me in that one sniff, and the physical pain in my body it left me for a few moments. I put the blanket in the car boot and had one last sniff, "Bloody weirdo!" said Vale, and he was back! Sitting next to me, looking disapprovingly up at me, still missing his left cancerous ear and one big remaining floppy ear on his right.

After several sessions with the therapist, I declared I don't know how this works, but I seemed to be sorting my head out I lied. "I don't see my dog anymore, and I'm feeling much calmer," I said. He was sat next to her and frowned at me, 'You lying fat bastard,' he whispered, then spoke to me as we left the room, 'You're as mad as a box of frogs, dad!'"

He was a potty mouth, and I don't know where he got it from – do you? We have a new sarcastic dog now, a girl from Cyprus named Leera. She's lying next to me now. Very occasionally, she sounds and looks like my boy, just the odd tell-tale signs; I like to think that he's still with me when I need him the most, just like Stuart Little the mouse did while in hospital (drum roll...)

Counselling left me frustrated. I'm fickle, and seeing a pretty lady for an hour every week on its own was nice but hugely stressful too, especially the trying to work out what to say part, and more importantly, what not to say. I do intend to try again and be more honest about it.

I was then referred to a Stress management course over six weeks after work. I say after work, but it was at a time that would be after work for most people. 5.30 for me meant I'd arrive stressed with the pressure of rushing to be on time, with a cup of coffee in hand too, only to find out in week four that caffeine needed to go! I stayed with it, and 5 weeks later, the course finished as planned. I quite enjoyed the weekly get-togethers; I even took notes!

I had come to see a counsellor after visiting my GP in tears. I was depressed most days and just miserable. I wanted help. I'd planned to kill myself again following a horrible encounter with a bully at work – the bastard. The antidepressants were meant to make me feel 'better', but they weren't working either. The doctor explained how difficult it would be to get me a mental health referral because I wasn't at risk or harmed. I eventually received a 'specialist assessment', but the nurse I saw said that I wasn't really trying to kill myself. The most they could offer was counselling. So the penny dropped; if I wanted medical help for my mental health, I needed to either lie or kill myself. A bit odd, but that has been my experience. Unless I was all but dead, no help was coming for me. I will try again, though, as I find myself getting darker and darker again through the lockdowns.

Chapter 17: Adoption

Starting a family and having kids is one of the biggest and most important decisions any of us can make in life. It is also one of the most satisfying. Shana and I had been together for a few years and were talking about having children. We both mentioned how unfair it was that so many children in the world have already been born but, for whatever reason, no longer had a family to take care of them and love them. We both agreed that we'd like to adopt a child. We have no strong views opposing anyone's personal choice to start a family through conception. We both just felt that how could we justify that approach when there were children at our 'doorstep' who needed a family? This was about seven years before my stroke.

We decided to apply to be considered through our local authority at the time in Lancashire. In the end, after four years of processes, form filling and meeting, we found our future daughter. The delay was terrible, but I'd never discourage anyone from adopting. We hope things have changed beyond recognition now, as back then, (14 years) it was an unnecessarily protracted process. The Local Authority are effectively the parent of children who are 'placed' for adoption. Therefore, it is understandable how much information and checks they need to carry out before placing the life of 'their' child into the responsibility of relative strangers, but it felt out of touch. There are thousands of children in the UK who need a new family through adoption at any point in time.

I found the process frustrating and slow, and once we started in the procedure and told friends, it was amazing that many people we already knew had started on the same journey themselves once. But due to the way the process works, they had withdrawn from it. Sure, some people won't be suitable, and people will pull out through a process of self-selection. Indeed there has to be a better way? Money and education are no guarantee of a person's suitability or stability to become an adoptive parent. More so, the process of questionnaires and weekly interviews were mind-numbingly repetitive. I don't believe you can mitigate against every risk, and there are well-reported failures in the press of apparently respectable people in society who go on to cause further harm to the children. 'It made no sense to extend it to 4 years for the adoption to be 'approved'.

Our application was threatened to be stalled on several occasions: we needed a bathroom fitter; apparently, this would be too disruptive to our lives, according to the Social Worker. Then, we got a dog (Vale) and the Social Worker wanted to halt the processes – we'd hired a dog trainer and joined a kennel club dog training scheme, which is far more than most people would do in a 'regular' circumstance. I worry how many potential great adoptive parents are put off through a system that tries to protect against every conceivable scenario. The most bizarre part was measuring the gaps of our stair rails! And a questionnaire on our household electrics. I'm surprised they didn't insist that we have a bag of salt if it ever snowed or that we must purchase a new Volvo in case we were ever in a car crash. Then once we did adopt, they gave us about £50 to help with costs (a Car seat), then dropped us like a hot potato.

After being 'approved', we had to attend a panel and faced some strange questions. We lived in an apartment at the time, and the panel of 'experts' wanted to know how we'd manage with a young child and carrying in the shopping to our first-floor home? I nearly fell off my chair; this was their big concern? How did they think people live in proper city centers? Do they believe they remain childless? Following approval, we weren't matched with any children. I became frustrated after a year. Finally, our Social Worker, Jane (real name) told us that we just had to be more patient. By chance, Channel 4 TV had a program on adoption and produced a leaflet featuring children from across the country who needed a new home.

We enquired, and after enquiring about five different children, we thought we could become mum and dad. We were excited and checked the post and email every day. It was hugely disappointing to find that the leaflet contained children from our local council area, but we applied anyway.

"Mr. WOODFORD if you could please call us about your enquiry about the adoption of [name]," called out the voice mail on our phone as we arrived home from work. I phoned the following morning, "You've been approved for a year and completed several months of volunteering in a children's center? Can I be blunt, is there something you're not telling me? You both sound ideal, and we have children today that you'd be a potential match for," said the SW from London. She went on to explain, "But for this particular child we do believe they should be placed with a black family." We were disappointed, but we understood and I probably agree.

"Philip," started the next call, "I'm disappointed that you didn't tell me that you were both applying for children from around the country!" said our Social Worker, I responded with "this is a national campaign, and your authority is part of the campaign, you should know about and have told us, we found out from the TV, unacceptable Jane," I complained, getting angry over the phone, finishing with, "I don't think you're representing us very well. It's been a year, and we've heard nothing from you, yet there is a child in our county featured as part of a TV programme, and you didn't let us know about it!" Jane incredulously responded with "You want me to let you know about every child?" She asked. I was fuming; I could feel myself burning up in anger, but I kept my calm. "Yes, I do. You're providing a service, you're paid to keep us updated, so yes, we want to know." Down went the phone!

I became calmer but struggled when we met the week later as we'd heard from other Social Workers across the country interested in us as well as the Social Worker for the child in our authority area, but still not from our Social Worker. It wasn't a comfortable meeting. "You're not doing a good job I told her," keeping calm and breathing slowly. "Philip, you are not our priority, it's the children." I laughed as I replied, "If they were your priority, you'd be matching them with new families. Did you know your colleague [name removed] has called us about a child we enquired about following the TV programme, and she only lives 30 minutes away! And she wants to meet you too about it." We all agreed that our Social Worker would make contact with the other Social Worker and obtain the details. We weren't going to give in that easy when the future happiness and security of a child was at stake. I was too nervous about submitting a formal complaint, but I should have.

13 years on and our eldest daughter is now nearly 17. She was kept in foster care for almost 4 years unnecessarily and had to endure the harm and pain of saying goodbye to the foster careers she loved as mum and dad since birth. It turned out that apparently, our Social Worker did know about her but had decided against telling us years earlier for reasons only she will know. I remain convinced it was an outdated

bias on her behalf. She called me naive once I when said I could love and care for a terminally ill or disabled child. How dare she decide how I felt or cope based on her training 30 years earlier before even mobile phones were invented. I'm sure it would have ripped me apart to see a child die, but together, 'Shana and I would have ensured whatever time they had with us would have been as positive and as loving as possible.

I've delivered several talks to prospective adoptive parents over the last 15 years. My daughters gave me this list of things that an adoptive child needs:

Love;

Safety; and an

IPhone!

Kids are perceptive, and I often think that the assessments for adoptive parents should be undertaken by children, not solely Social Workers. However, in my experience, you can't 'kid a kidder', and children see through the bullshit much better.

The positives have outshone all the difficult times and poor experience of applying to adopt, so much so that we did it again. It was with a different authority this time (Cumbria), and was a great experience. The Social Worker, Janneke (real Name) was down to earth and could hold a regular, non-contrived conversation just about anything in life, and she got the very best out of us. Our second daughter was ten months old when she came to us. She's now 11 and a beautiful, fun, handful! We are currently looking to move home again and buy a bigger house so we can perhaps adopt one more child, as adoptive children can't share a bedroom according to our local authority dogooders, in the voice of Jim Royle from the Royal Family nice and loudly say, "My arse!." I've read the books explaining the reasons and disagree with it. All good intentions, but impractical for real life and a needless obstruction for a child gaining a new family.

I'd recommend the adoption experience to anyone willing. I believe our first poor experience was about a person and was not indicative of the whole authority. We, of course, have spoken to many other adoptive parents, and sadly, it wasn't isolated either.

Chapter 18: Westminster Bridge

It was 22 March 2017; it had been a fun morning. Maria (real name so she can say she's in a book!) and I were meeting our boss, the CEO and the chairman in London, we were all to meet with a group of MPs. It's something I arranged most years. MPs are incredibly busy, and diaries conflict between them all. Therefore, we organised a day to visit them at Parliament and brief them on how the hospitals are performing and the issues and challenges we were facing. It's not a 'pitch'. There aren't reports produced or presentations.

This day was starting fun as Maria, and I had about an hour before we were to meet at Portcullis House. The administrative building opposite the Houses of Parliament. It is a modern building on the banks of the Thames that housed multiple floors of meeting rooms, and on the ground floor, bright daylight and tree-lined atrium with food court and coffee shops. We decided to grab some food first and went into a pub. It was next door to Portcullis House; very quaint, just what you'd hope for as a tourist in London, bustling full of businesspeople and thick exposed wooden beams, all quite traditional. I was still using a walking stick at this time and was still unstable. I was six months post-hospital discharge and suffering from elements of PTSD. We pushed our way through the crowds and eventually found a

243

table. Maria is a lovely person, kind and thoughtful. It is always a privilege to spend time with her. We had 30 minutes to go but forced a pint and fish and chips down our necks!

We met an unhappy CEO outside of Portcullis house, having reached a minute late but no longer hungry. There was a long queue as always, into the building, but this felt extra slow and long. I phoned one of the MPs I knew who came out with his ID pass and escorted us to the front of the queue. It's a high-security building, so you still need to go through airline-style security with the police stood there, looking menacing with machine guns. The meeting had Maria, the CEO and Chair, three MPs, and an administrator or two. It was a corner office on the 2nd floor, overlooking Westminster Bridge, the Thames, and the Houses of Parliament. It was an iconic and memorable view; a photographer or painter would love this spot.

The meeting was going well with a good healthy discussion. I don't know why but I looked up across the table and out of the window to the Bridge. It was strangely quiet, and I could see what looked like people crowded around a person on the pavement. As I looked up the bridge, I could see some people in yellow hi-viz jackets, not moving. They just stood there, and the blue lights of an ambulance flashed across them.

A bell rang in the room – this was quite normal to hear as it signals it is time for the MPs to go and vote on a 'bill', and the MPs stood up, apologised and explained they had to go to vote. One MP left, and another answered their mobile (I've decided to preserve their confidence and not talk about names or what I heard them say). The other people had rushed to the side window and started shouting that a car had crashed into the wall outside.

The next hour was a bit hurried and blurry as we were effectively locked in a room. A person came to the door to tell us we had to stay where we were. I could hear screaming and panic outside the door, and with different people coming to the door, we heard different rumours, such as of a gunman in the building. We were all shocked and frightened. I felt unable to protect myself at that moment, and a thousand what-ifs flooded my mind; I needed a hug! We closed the door and stayed where we were. The only news we were now getting was on the TV, and the BBC correspondent, Laura Kuensberg. One of the people in the room, encouraged us all to keep away from the windows – a bit of very sensible advice. I thought, but those words didn't make me feel much calmer. My boss kept checking on me. I was worried and reticent. A colleague was now sat on the floor, worried. A security guard came to the door to tell us we were to evacuate downstairs, and then as we exited the room into the corridor, we were ushered back into the room. It was a little chaotic, but you wouldn't think this was a high-security government building with a 'plan' for such eventualities. Maria, bless her, this was her first business trip away with us. The attack had happened at about 14:40, according to the news reports.

As per reports, this is what happened (I've changed the attackers' name to 'Terrorist' as I don't believe in giving them any further notoriety):

82-second attack

https://www.bbc.com/news/uk-39355108

14:40:08 – [The Terrorist] car mounts pavement on Westminster Bridge and hits pedestrians

14:40:38 - [The Terrorist] crashes into the perimeter fence of Palace of Westminster

14:40:59 - First 999 call made to Met police

14:41:30 - [The Terrorist] leaves vehicle, runs towards Parliament and is shot dead

I think it must have been about 4 pm before we were led downstairs. I wasn't allowed to use the elevator. My boss and Maria looked after me to help me down the stairs. I fought back the tears – I still cried daily – which was a hangover of the stroke. We were taken to a part of the ground floor to wait and were then hurriedly moved to another part of the building. The security guard explained there was a fear there might be an explosive in the crashed car on the side of the building we were being held in. We were taken to what felt like a hallway to sit in. It was all austere and dark wood with uncomfortable seats. We had all been receiving calls on our mobile phones from family. I'd posted on Facebook that morning that I was in Parliament buildings, so I posted an "I'm ok" message. There was a toilet to use, but we were not given any hot drinks or food to eat despite there being a food court in the building! Someone found a vending machine and water was purchased and thankfully handed around. I'd already started to drink water out of my hands from the sink in the toilet. We stayed locked in the building until about 9.30 pm. The whole of the Westminster area had been understandably 'locked down' by the police.

The police eventually led us out through an underground tunnel and up into the Palace of Westminster by the police. It was a tricky walk in the dark and cold with a walking stick to Kings Cross train station. The tube station had been sealed off, and due to the lockdown perimeter, no taxis were available. I hobbled there, making the last train home with Maria. We were quiet on the journey north. After hours of utter disbelief, we were lucky enough to have made it through. I'm glad Maria was with me.

Chapter 19: Ladies of the Night

This is the most challenging part of the book for me. To give the end away, I do 'sleep' with a prostitute, but not in the way you think. One story is a little uncomfortable to share, however, as I did not want to identify anyone by mistake, so I've again excluded dates and changed names.

My first encounter with a prostitute was on my 16th birthday. My sister was driving. We had been out for a meal; me and my then girlfriend were in the back of the car. My sister pulled the car over on the way back from my dinner out. She got out of the car and a woman standing on the corner came over. The next thing I know, they talked, the lady was bent over with her head through my door window. She pulled her top down to show her breasts. They fell out right in front of me – it was just funny, really! My sister does make me laugh.

Once when I was a long-distance driver, probably aged 22, I remember sleeping outside of Poole in Dorset one night. I would sleep in the back of the van in my sleeping bag and duvet, on top of the parcels! There was a knock on the van side door and I opened it. A girl no more than 16 of whose description at most I'd say, 'tarted up', with thick makeup and messy hair, a jacket which showed she only had a bra on underneath, was offering me a blow job for a tenner (£10). I declined but said I would pay her to spend the night with me in the van and have a can of beer with me, but that I wasn't paying her for sex. So she stayed the night, we cuddled, she left. I hope I kept her from being abused that night. I just wanted to keep her safe and enjoy her company. I've thought about her a lot over the years and what might have become of her and the family that was missing their baby girl.

The city of Amsterdam was even better than I hoped, and I loved it – still do. In fact, I love all of Holland, full stop. The culture suits me, along with the cycling way of life. I have visited a few times to cycle, including with my family and hopefully I will again in 2022, pandemic permitting. The red light district is a bit odd, but strangely entertaining and 'safe' too. The 'special' cake was most relaxing! The rest of the group were sat around tables along the canal outside a bar with a road separating the canal, then a drinking area and then pavement. I sat for what felt like hours with a pint of beer, sipping it in the sun on the roadside. Everything went numb. I think I was asleep until a car passing behind me glanced the back of my head! I can't recall which one of the stag party's it was (honest!), but we lost him for three days; he found a prostitute he couldn't get enough of and never came back!

The three of us visited a red-light window. A woman was leaning against the doorway in white lingerie, looking incredible. We chatted with her on the doorstep of the 'shop' before accepting her offer to come in and talk to her inside. None of us intended for anything else to happen, and certainly not sexual. We were the 'boring' members of the trip, the 'squares' saying how bad it was for the women, whilst the rest of the lads jeered and whistled at them. We were naïve indeed because we were given a bucket and a cloth to wash our privates as soon as the three of us went in. There was no way I was having sex with anyone, and certainly not with two blokes stood by me!

We were in a small room of what would have once been a house living room with stairs leading upstairs and then a large bay window area and lots of pillows and blankets. It was dimly lit but strangely not red! The lady handed a laminated price list to us – I don't know why but it seemed all seemed perfectly normal. It must have been the copious amounts of Dutch beer and space cakes rushing around my body that altered my sense of 'normal'! After about a minute or so, a hulk-sized man came down the stairs into the front of the 'shop' and closed the window blinds. He was twice the width as a normal man with a neck as wide as my thighs! At the back of the shop was an alcove with what looked like a doctor's couch. I assume this was his bed. The man was dressed in a black suit, shirt, and tie. He then stood next to the door with one thick ape-like arm and hand against it. The lady called upstairs, and a less 'attractive' lady came down – the other lady was the 'bait' I realised.

The new lady sat in an armchair in front of the three of us. She opened her legs wide and draped them over the arms of the chair on either side, and invited us all to join her. She beckoned us to come closer. We all looked at the minder at the door and knew we were about to be beaten up. You could just sense it. We could also hear talking and footsteps from upstairs. We went to leave before it was too late, and the big man just smiled and moved out of the way and put out his hand out like a beggar. His hands were like shovels. I could imagine them wrapped around my throat if we didn't put money into them. We didn't argue, we all gave him some money and made a quick exit! No beating for us; it was a strange night but thinking about it makes me laugh. It's no life, is it, for these ladies?

At the end of the day

I can't blame my dad for my feelings forever. I'm old enough to take responsibility for my life now, and I have. Yesterday was then, but tomorrow and today are yet to happen, and they are in my control. I've still got lots of dreams and hopes, some of them daft, some exciting, others less so… but they are all mine and I am in control.

A funny thing happened while writing this. Some people from the local NHS contacted me once they learned of the book – funny how nobody reached out about my mental health despite the blurb on my website being clear it was about that too. They instead wanted to know what I might

251

reveal about the maternity scandal. Yes, I've some 'scandal' I could have shared, but this isn't the way to do it, yet.

Chapter 20: The Missing Chapter

I thought long and hard about whether or not to include this chapter. Clearly, I haven't!

This missing chapter was a detailed list of allegations by me. I've talked about going off to take my own life recently at a train station in Birmingham, only I haven't been completely honest or authentic in my explanation. The truth is: I believe that I was being bullied and harassed at work, and I couldn't take it anymore. I did try to get help, but that only made the situation much worse. I should have been stronger than the person I asked to help, as they were weak and capitulated to an outdated hierarchy that wields power through threats and denigrating them in return: essentially cowards. I deeply regret I didn't stick to my convictions as these people can now go on to cause damage to other people.

These allegations would have exposed me to libel action as I can't fully prove them. While I have independent supporting information and records of meeting contents, they are my view of how it felt; I now need less stress in my life, not more. I will do all I can now to prevent them from causing others harm. I don't believe that raising my accusations in detail in this book would have me getting any further support or help; based on my experience of seeking help, I firmly believe the opposite. I think that all that would have happened is I would have received a solicitor's letter and then a long period of further stress and anxiety. So I wrote a chapter chronologically detailing all of the events with evidence, not just accusations, and I feel better for doing so. But then at the last minute, I deleted it for another day! Maybe it will appear on my blog one day…? Who knows?

Until then, goodbye and sleep well, Vale. X

The end, until next time

Phil x

That's it, it's finished you can go now!

I am available for talks about my life and surviving my stroke, you can contact me at:

www.philwoodford.co.uk

Twitter: Phil_woodford

E: woodfordp@clara.co.uk

You can also see me on YouTube: https://youtu.be/QiXpvR1nPjg

i Krav Maga is a military self-defence and fighting system developed for the Israel Defense Forces (IDF) and Israeli security forces derived from a combination of techniques sourced from Boxing, Wrestling, Judo, Aikido, and Karate. Krav Maga is known for its focus on real-world situations and its extreme efficiency.

Lightning Source UK Ltd.
Milton Keynes UK
UKHW051023080722
405563UK00006B/128